BHARATIYA SAKSHYA ADHINIYAM

MR. PIYUSH ARORA

Made with ♥ on the Notion Press Platform
www.notionpress.com

BHARATIYA SAKSHYA ADHINIYAM

BY MR PIYUSH ARORA

STUDENT OF UPES , DEHRADUN

I Dedicate To my parents, Satish Arora and Swati Arora, whose unwavering support and guidance have been the cornerstone of all my endeavors. To all the students and legal practitioners who strive for knowledge and justice, may this work be a useful companion in your journey.

Contents

Foreword

The law is a living entity, constantly evolving and adapting to the needs of society. The Indian Evidence Act, or Bharatiya Sakshya Adhiniyam, is no exception. It stands as a pillar in the Indian legal system, guiding the principles of justice and fairness. This book has been written with the intent to illuminate the intricate facets of evidence law in India, making it accessible to both students and professionals alike. It is my hope that this work will serve as a valuable resource in understanding and applying the principles enshrined in the Act. As we navigate through the complexities of legal evidence, may this book provide clarity, insight, and a deeper appreciation for the rule of law.

Preface

The journey of writing this book, Bharatiya Sakshya Adhiniyam, has been both challenging and fulfilling. The Indian Evidence Act, 1872, is a cornerstone of our legal system, yet its intricacies often present challenges to students and practitioners alike. My aim in writing this book is to simplify these complexities and present the principles of evidence law in a manner that is both comprehensive and accessible.

Throughout this book, I have endeavored to maintain a balance between theoretical discussions and practical applications, ensuring that readers not only understand the law but also how it is applied in real-world scenarios. I have drawn from various judicial pronouncements, legislative amendments, and scholarly interpretations to provide a well-rounded perspective on the subject.

This book is the culmination of countless hours of research, reflection, and writing. It is intended to be a reliable companion for students, legal practitioners, and anyone with an interest in the field of evidence law. I hope that this work will inspire a deeper understanding and appreciation of the Indian legal system and contribute positively to the study and practice of law.

I extend my sincere gratitude to my mentors, colleagues, and family, whose support has been instrumental in the completion of this book. Any errors or omissions are entirely my own, and I welcome constructive feedback from readers to improve future editions.

Acknowledgements

Writing this book, Bharatiya Sakshya Adhiniyam, has been a rewarding experience, made possible by the guidance and support of many individuals. I am deeply grateful to my parents, Satish Kumar Arora and Swati Arora, whose constant encouragement and belief in my abilities have been my greatest source of strength.

I would like to extend my heartfelt thanks to my professors and mentors, who have instilled in me a deep appreciation for the law and have guided me throughout my academic journey. Their insights and teachings have greatly influenced the content and direction of this book.

I am also indebted to my friends and colleagues, who have provided invaluable feedback and support during the writing process. Their constructive criticism has helped shape this book into a comprehensive resource for students and legal practitioners.

Special thanks go to Notion Press for their support in bringing this book to publication, and to all those who have contributed in ways both big and small to the completion of this work.

Finally, I wish to acknowledge the many legal scholars, jurists, and authors whose work has served as a foundation for this book. Their contributions to the field of law have been instrumental in my own understanding and interpretation of the Indian Evidence Act.

To everyone who has been a part of this journey, thank you. This book would not have been possible without your unwavering support.

Prologue

The law is often perceived as a complex web of rules and regulations, yet at its core, it serves the simple and profound purpose of ensuring justice. The Indian Evidence Act, 1872, is one such crucial piece of legislation, defining the boundaries of what is acceptable as evidence in our courts of law. This book, Bharatiya Sakshya Adhiniyam, is an attempt to unravel the intricacies of this Act, making it accessible to both the seasoned practitioner and the eager student.

As we embark on this exploration, it is important to remember that evidence law is not just about technicalities—it is about truth. The principles laid down in the Act are designed to sift through the noise and bring forth clarity, allowing the courts to make informed decisions based on facts. This book aims to illuminate these principles, offering a clear path through the sometimes daunting landscape of legal evidence.

In this prologue, I wish to set the stage for what lies ahead: a journey through the heart of evidence law, where each chapter builds upon the last, leading to a comprehensive understanding of the subject. Whether you are a student preparing for examinations, a lawyer looking to sharpen your skills, or simply someone with a keen interest in the law, this book is for you.

As we delve into the chapters that follow, let us keep in mind the ultimate goal of this Act—to uphold justice by ensuring that the truth prevails.

CHAPTER ONE

PRELIMINARY

1. Short title, application and commencement.—(1) This Act may be called the Bharatiya Sakshya Adhiniyam, 2023.

2) It applies to all judicial proceedings in or before any Court, including Courts-martial, but not to affidavits presented to any Court or officer, nor to proceedings before an arbitrator.

(3) It shall come into force on such date as the Central Government may, by notification in the Official Gazette, appoint.

COMMENT

The comment mentioned under Section 1 of the Bharatiya Sakshya Adhiniyam, 2023 are based upon Section 1 of the Indian Evidence Act, 1872 (1 of 1872)

A domestic enquiry is not bound by technical rules of Evidence Act, 1872, however, the substantive rules of natural justice could not be ignored by domestic tribunal.

Central Bank of India v. P.C. Jain, AIR 1969 SC 983.

2. Definitions.— (1) In this Adhiniyam, unless the context otherwise requires,-

(a)"Court" includes all Judges and Magistrates, and all persons, except arbitrators, legally authorised to take evidence;.

(b) "conclusive proof" means when one fact is declared by this Adhiniyam to be conclusive proof of another, the Court shall, on proof of the one fact, regard the other as proved, and shall not allow evidence to be given for the purpose of disproving it;

(c) "disproved" in relation to a fact, means when, after considering the matters before it, the Court either believes that it does not exist, or considers its non-existence so probable that a prudent man ought, under thecircumstances of the particular case, to act upon the supposition that it does not exist;

(d) "document" means any matter expressed or described or otherwise recorded upon any substance by means of letters, figures or marks or any other means or by more than one of those means, intended to be used, or which may be used, for the purpose of recording that matter and includes electronic and digital records.

Illustrations

(i) A writing is a document.

(ii) Words printed, lithographed or photographed are documents.

iii) A map or plan is a document.

(iv) An inscription on a metal plate or stone is a document.

(v) A caricature is a document.

(vi) An electronic record on emails, server logs, documents on computers, laptop or smartphone, messages, websites, locational evidence and voice mail messages stored on digital devices are documents;

(e) "evidence" means and includes—

(i) all statements including statements given electronically which the Court permits or requires to be made before it by witnesses in relation to matters of fact under inquiry and such statements are called oral evidence;

(ii) all documents including electronic or digital records produced for the inspection of the Court and such documents are called documentary evidence;

According to stephen , the word evidence is used in three senses:

1. words uttered and thing exhibit in court
2. facts proved by those words or things , which are regarded as ground word of inference as to other facts not so proved , and
3. relevancy of a particular fact to matter under inquiry

Bentham :- defines evidence as " any matter of fact , the effect , tendency or design of which when presented to the mind , is to produce in the mind a persuasion concerning the existence of some other matter of fact – a persuasion either affirmative or disaffirmative of its existence . one of the two facts so connected , the latter may be distinguished as the principal fact and the former as the evidentiary fact ."

taylor uses the word " evidence " to mean " all the legal means exclusive of mere argument which tend to prove or disprove any fact the truth of which is submitted to judicial investigation

the fundamental rules of evidence are:-

1. evidence must be confined to the matters in issue
2. hearsay evidence is not to be admitted .
3. in all cases , the best evidence must be given

Types of Evidences

Best evidence – the best evidence or the original evidence means the primary evidence

Circumstantial evidence :- circumstantial evidence means the evidence of circumstancers and is sometimes referred to as presumptive evidence .

suppose a is charged with the murder of b . at the trial a witnesses c, on behalf of the prosecution , gives evidence that he saw a stab

b. or , c may make the statement that he saw a running away from the place where b corpse was found , with a blood strained knife in his hand . in the first case the evidence given by c is usually referred to as direct evidence and in the second , as circumstantial evidence . because , c makes a statement about a circumstance , a relevant fact which if believed , may convince the court of the guilt of a , therefore , we might say that when evidence isgiven ofcircumstances , or relevant facts , from which an inference may be drawn about the fact in issue , then it is called circumstantial evidence .

kotari suri vs state of orissa ,1984 cr. l.j.noc 122

circumstantial evidence means a fact on which an inference is to be founded . the firm must be closely knitted and must carry conviction the mind of a judge

makkan lal vs state of rajasthan

it is laid down that circumstances should be like a spider web . there must not be any exit way.

tests :-

it is well settled down that when a case rests on circumstantial evidence , such evidence must satisfy three tests :

1. the circumstances from which an inference of guilt is sought to be pointing drawn , must be cogently and firmly established .
2. those circumstances should be of a definite tendency unerringly pointing towards the guilt of the accussed .
3. the circumstances , taken cummulatively , should form a chain so complete that thereisno escape from the conclusion that within all Human Probability The Crime Was Committed By The Accused And Non Else .

CORROBORATIVE EVIDENCE & SUBSTANTIVE EVIDENCE

Corroborative evidence must be taken along with substantive evidence. When evidence is given of the fact in issue or of a relevant fact that is called substantive evidence. There are, however, several statements oral &documentary, which are not substantive evidence. They are not admissible by themselves, but become admissible to corroborate, or support, substantive evidence already given.

DIRECT EVIDENCE

The word direct evidence is used in two senses (a) as opposed to Hearsay evidence (b) as opposed to circumstantial evidence. In the first sense direct evidence is the evidence of a fact actually perceived by a witness with his own senses or an opinion held by him. And in the second sense direct evidence is that which goes expressly to the very point in question & proves it, if believed, without aid from inference or deductive reasoning, e.g. eye-witness, to a murder is direct evidence.

In jurisprudence, however, direct evidence is commonly used in a secondary sense,

viz. as limited to cases where the principal fact, or factum probandum, is attested directly by witnesses, things or documents.

INDIRECT EVIDENCE

Known in forensic procedure by the name of circumstantial evidence, is either conclusive or presumptive: Conclusive, where the connection between the principal & evidentiary facts - the factus probandum & the factum probans - is a necessary consequence of the laws of Nature: presumptive, where it only rests on a greater or less degree of probability.

Suppose A is charged with the murder of B by stabbing him. C, D, E, F, G & H are witnesses called by the prosecution. C says he saw A stab B. D says he heard B cry out that A was stabbing him. E says that he saw A running away with a blood-stained knife & blood-stained clothes. F says that he saw A washing his blood-stained clothes. G is a doctor who says that the knife found in A's possession might have caused the wounds found on B & H says that he heard from C, that C saw A stabbing

B. If we use the phrases direct evidence & circumstantial evidence, the evidence

given by C is direct evidence & that given by the others, circumstantial evidence, because C gives evidence of the very matter in controversy, whereas D to H give evidence of circumstances which, if believed, would assist the court in drawing an inference about the matter in controversy. But, if we use direct evidence as used in Section 60, then the evidence of C to G is direct evidence & that of H is indirect evidence. Because each of them, C to G, is giving evidence about a fact which was perceived by him by the particular sense by which it was capable of being perceived;

Whereas, H alone is talking about A stabbing B - a fact capable of being seen, but without seeing it. He has heard about it. The evidence sought to be given by H is also called hearsay evidence & in general, is not admissible in a court of law. Direct evidence is used in the Act in contrast to hearsay evidence. It is also referred to sometimes as original evidence. Hearsay evidence, indirect evidence & derivative evidence mean the same thing.

HEARSAY EVIDENCE

Stephen says, "the word 'hearsay' is used in various senses. Sometimes, it means whatever a person is heard to say; sometimes it means whatever a person declares on information given by some one else; sometimes it is treated as nearly synonymous with 'irrelevant'."

It is the fundamental rule of the English Law of Evidence that Hearsay is not admissible. The reasons why hearsay evidence is not received as relevant evidence are:

a) the person giving such evidence does not feel any responsibility. If he is cornered he has a line of escape by saying "do not know, but so & so told me";

b) truth is diluted & diminished with each repetition; and

c) if permitted, gives ample scope for playing fraud by saying "someone told me that ....".

It would be attaching importance to a false rumour flying from one foul lip to another.

demeanour of witness can not be seen so there is possibility that reality can not be seen.

e) The original maker of statement can not be cross-examined.

Exception to Hearsay evidence:

Res-gestae

Admission

Dying declaration -

Confession

Confidential evidence

Statements given in other judicial proceedings
opinion of author when relevant.

Rationale behind these exceptions:

1) Necessity because person not available
2) Relevancy

Hearsay evidence when admissible:

R.V. Raoji , 6 Bom. L.R. 34

Where the object of the legislature is simply to provide preventive measures, evidence of repute though hearsay, is admissible.

Ganauri V.R., 16 C 210

Certain communications though hearsay, where held admissible in cross examination in so far as they relate to the question of the credibility of the witness.

Muni Lal Gupta vs. State 1988 Cr. L.J. 627, 630

The witness was aroused on hearing the cries of two other prosecution witnesses that the accused had killed the children. His evidence of what he heard is admissible.

ORAL EVIDENCE & DOCUMENTARY EVIDENCE

If it is a case of oral evidence, the Act requires that only that person who has actually perceived something by that sense by which it is capable of perception, should make the statement about it & no one else.

If it is documentary evidence, the Act requires that ordinarily the original should be produced, because a copy may contain omission or mistakes of a deliberate or accidental nature.

Documentary evidence is defined in the Act as: All documents produced for the inspection of the court. The purpose of producing documents, is to rely upon the truth of the statement contained therein. This involves, when a document is produced in court, the examination of three questions; (i) is the document genuine, (ii) what are its contents & (iii) are the statements in the document true?

By real evidence is meant evidence of which, any object belonging to the class of things, is the source, person also being included in respect of such properties as belong to them in common with things. This sort of evidence may be either immediate, where the thing comes under the cognizance of our senses: or reported, where its evidence is related to us by others. Personal evidence is that which is afforded by a human agent, either by way of discourse or by voluntary signs.

Suppose a letter is produced as having been written by A & it contains a statement that B murdered C. Thethree questions are: (i) is the letter written by A? (ii) what does letter contain? and (iii) is the statement that B murdered C true?

PRIMARY & SECONDARY EVIDENCE

We can easily understand it by way of above given example. In the above example, the first & third questions can be answered by calling A as a witness. But the second can normally be answered only by providing the letter. When the original letter is produced, it is said that primary evidence of the contents if given. When a copy is permitted & such copy is produced to prove the contents of a document;

secondary evidence is said to be given of the contents.

Primary evidence: Primary evidence means the document itself produced for the inspection of the Court.

Explanation 1: Where a document is executed in several parts, each part is primary evidence of the document; where a document is executed in counterpart, each counterpart being executed by one or some of the parties only, each counterpart is primary evidence as against the parties executing it.

Explanation 2: Where a number of documents are all made by one uniform process, as in the case of printing, lithography, or photography, each is primaryevidence of the contents of the rest; but, where they are all copiesof a common original, they are not primary evidence of the contents of the original.

Illustration

A person is shown to have been in possession of a number of placards, all printed at one time from one original. Any one of the placards is primary evidence of the contents of any other, but no one of them is primary evidence of the contents of the original.

Secondary evidence: Secondary evidence means and includes -

a. Certified copies given under the provisions hereinafter contained;

b) Copies made from the original by mechanical processes which in themselves insure the accuracy of the copy, and copies compared with such copies;

c) Copies made from or compared with the original;

a. Counterparts of documents as against the parties who did not execute them;

e) Oral accounts of the contents of a document given by some person who has himself seen it.

Illustration

i) A photograph of an original is secondary evidence of its contents, though the two have not been compared, if it is proved that the thing photographed was the original.

ii) A copy compared with a copy of a letter made by a copying machine is secondary evidence of the contents of the letter, if it is shown that the copy made by the copying machine was made from the original.

iii) A copy transcribed from a copy, but afterwards compared with the original, is secondary evidence; but the copy not so compared is not secondary evidence of the original, although the copy from which it was transcribed was compared with the original.

iv) Neither an oral account of a copy compared with the original, nor an oral account of a photograph or machine-copy of the original, is secondary evidence of the original.

The genuineness of a document or the truth of its contents are proved either by primary or by secondary evidence.

ORIGINAL EVIDENCE

The original is that which a witness reports himself so have been or heard through the medium of his own senses.

REAL & PERSONAL EVIDENCE

It refers to any matter which the court perceives itself e.g. that a man standing before a judge has got a scar on his face, objects like murder weapon, blood-stained clothes, photographs etc.

CONCLUSIVE EVIDENCE

Where the connection between the principal & evidentiary fact is a necessary conclusion.

(f)"fact" means and includes—

(i) any thing, state of things, or relation of things, capable of being perceived by the senses;

(ii) any mental condition of which any person is conscious.

Illustrations

i) That there are certain objects arranged in a certain order in a certain place, is a fact.

(ii) That a person heard or saw something, is a fact. (iii) That a person said certain words, is a fact.

(iv) That a person holds a certain opinion, has a certain intention, acts in good faith, or fraudulently, or uses a particular word in a particular sensation, is a fact;

sense, or is or was at a specified time conscious of a particular

(g) "facts in issue" means and includes any fact from which, either by itself or in connection with other facts, the existence, non-existence, nature or extent of any right,liability or disability, asserted or denied in any suit or proceeding, necessarily follows.

Explanation.- Whenever, under the provisions of the law for the time being in force relating to civil procedure, any Court records an issue of fact, the fact to be asserted or denied in the answer to such issue is a fact in issue.

Illustrations

A is accused of the murder of B. At his trial, the following facts may be in issue:-

(i) That A caused B's death.

(ii) That A intended to cause B's death.

(iii) That A had received grave and sudden provocation from B.

(iv) That A, at the time of doing the act which caused B's death, was, by reason of unsoundness of mind, incapable of knowing its nature;

(h) "may presume". —Whenever it is provided by this Adhiniyam that the Court may presume a fact, it may either regard such tact as proved, unless and until it is disproved or may call for proof of it;

(i) "not proved".—A fact is said to be not proved when it is neither proved nor disproved;

(i) "proved". —A fact is said to be proved when, after considering the matters before it, the Court either believes it to exist, or considers its existence so probable that a prudent man ought, under the circumstances of the particular case, to act upon the supposition that it exists;

(k) "relevant".—A fact is said to be relevant to another when it is connected with the other in any of the ways referred to in the provisions of this Adhiniyam relating to the relevancy of facts;

(I) "shall presume". —Whenever it is directed by this Adhiniyam that the Court shall presume a fact, it shall regard such fact as proved, unless and until it is disproved.

(2) Words and expressions used herein and not defined but defined in the Information Technology Act, 2000 (21 of 2000), the Bharatiya Nagarik Suraksha Sanita, 2023 and the Bharatiya Nyaya Sanita, 2023 shall have the same meanings as assigned to them in the said Act and Sanhitas.

COMMENT

The comment mentioned under Section 2 of the Bharatiya Sakshya Adhiniyam, 2023 are based upon Section 3 of the Indian Evidence Act, 1872 (1 of 1872)

Oral Testimony

Oral testimony may be classified into three categories, viz.:—

(i) Wholly reliable; ii) Wholly unreliable;

(iii) Neither wholly reliable nor wholly unreliable. The first two categories of cases may not pose serious difficulty for the court in arriving at its conclusion(s). However, in the third category of cases, the court has to be circumspect and look for corroboration of any material particulars by

of prudence.

reliable testimony, direct or circumstantial, as a requirement of the rule

Munna Lal v. State of Uttar Pradesh, AIR 2023 SC 634.

CHAPTER TWO

RELEVANCY OF FACTS

3. Evidence may be given of facts in issue and relevant facts.- Evidence may be given in any suit or proceeding of the existence or non-existence of every fact in issue and of such other facts as are hereinafter declared to be relevant, and of no others.

Explanation.—This section shall not enable any person to give evidence of a fact which he is disentitled to prove by any provision of the law for the time being in force relating to civil procedure.

Illustrations

(a) A is tried for the murder of B by beating him with a club with the intention of causing his death.

At A's trial the following facts are in issue:-A's beating B with the club;

A's causing B's death by such beating;

A's intention to cause B's death.

(b) A suitor does not bring with him, and have in readiness for production at the first hearing of the case, a bond on which he relies. This section does not enable him to produce the bond or prove its contents at a subsequent stage of the proceedings, otherwise than in accordance with theconditions prescribed by the Code of Civil Procedure.

Magraj Patodia v. R.K. Birla, AIR 1971 SC 1295

The fact that a document was procured by improper or even illegal means will not be a bar to its admissibility if it is relevant and its genuiness proved. But while examining the proof given as to its genuineness the circumstances under which it came to be produced into court have to be taken into consideration.

Ram Chander vs. State of Haryana SC

It is laid down that a judge is not a recording machine and spectator only.

Pushpa Devi vs. Madhavan 1987 SC

The only exception of this rule is that where after the alleged offence improper method have been used to obtain evidence for it and the judge is of the view that the prejudicial effect of such evidence would be out of proportion to its evidentiary value.

Inadmissibility of Evidence

Gyan Chand V. State of Raj., 1993 Cr.L.J., Raj.

The accused was found to be in possession of unauthorised opium. Search, seizure and further investigations were done by the same authority and the same being violative of the principles of criminal jurisprudence. It was held that the documents of the search and seizure were inadmissible in evidence.

- The explanation prohibits a party from claiming any relief upon facts or documents not stated by him in his pleading.

4. Relevancy of facts forming part of same transaction.-Facts which, though not in issue, are so connected with a fact in issue or a relevant fact as to form part of the same transaction, are relevant, whether they occurred at the same time and place or at different times and places.

Illustrations

(a) A is accused of the murder of B by beating him. Whatever was said or done by A or B or the bystanders at the beating, or so shortly before or after it as to form part of the transaction, is a relevant fact.

(b) A is accused of waging war against the Government of India by taking part in an armed insurrection in which property is destroyed, troops are attacked and jails are broken open. The occurrence of these facts is relevant, as forming part of the general transaction, though A may not have been present at all of them.

(c) A sues B for a libel contained in a letter forming part of a correspondence. Letters between the parties relating to the subject out of which the libel arose, and forming part contain the libel itself.

of the correspondence in which it is contained, are relevant facts, though they do not

(d) The question is, whether certain goods ordered from B were delivered to A. is a relevant fact.

The goods were delivered to several intermediate persons successively. Each delivery is a relevant fact.

The doctrine of Res gestae

Under English law, the facts form the part of same transaction is called res gestae.

Res-gestae means the things done or words spoken in the course of same transaction.

A transaction is a group of facts so connected together as to be referred to by a single legal name, as a crime, a contract, a wrong or any other subject of inquiry which may be in issue

Shyam Nandan Singh v. State of Bihar, 1991 Cr. L.J.

An FIR lodged soon after the incident by persons who witnessed it becomes a part of happening so it is under the purview of the doctrine of res-gestae.

Sawaldas v. State of Bihar, 1974 SC

A husband, his father and mother were prosecuted for the murder of his wife.

She cried for help as soon as she was pushed into the room. Her children who were playing outside in verandah exclaimed at the same time that their mother was being killed. The exclamations of the children were received through the evidence of the persons who heard them. It was admissible evidence because it was res gestae.

Gentela V. Rao v. State of AP, AIR 1996 SC

The statements of persons who were injured by burns by the act of the accused in setting fire to the bus in which they were travelling, though recorded by a Magistrate. Under expectations of death, were held to be not relevant there being a hap of time between recording the statements and incidents.

3. Statement made by person may be a part of same transaction

Conditions:

1) Statement must be contemporoeous.

2) It should be immediate.

COMMENT

The comment mentioned under Section 4 of the Bharatiya Sakshya Adhiniyam, 2023 are based upon Section 6 of the Indian Evidence Act, 1872 (1 of 1872)

Rule of res gestae

Principle embodied in Section 6 of Evidence Act is usually known as the rule of res gestae. What it means is that a fact which, though not in issue, is so connected with the fact in issue "as to form part of the same transaction" becomes relevant by itself. To form particular statement as part of the same transaction utterances must be simultaneous with the incident or substantial contemporaneous that is made either during or immediately before or after its occurrence.

Balu Sudam Khalde v. State of Maharashtra, AIR 2023 SC 1736.

5. Facts which are occasion, cause or effect of facts in issue or relevant facts.-Facts which are the occasion, cause or effect, immediate or otherwise, of relevant facts, or facts in issue, or which constitute the state of things under which they happened, or which afforded an opportunity for their occurrence or transaction, are relevant.

Illustrations

(a) The question is, whether A robbed B. The facts that, shortly before the robbery, B went to a fair with money inhis possession, and that he showed it, or mentioned the fact that he had it, to third persons, are relevant.

(b) The question is, whether A murdered B. Marks on the ground, produced by a struggle at or near the place where the murder was committed, are relevant facts.

(c) The question is, whether A poisoned B. The state of B's health before the symptoms ascribed to poison, and habits of B, known to A, which afforded an opportunity for the administration of poison, are relevant facts.

Yusuf Ali vs. State (1967) Bom LR

A contemporaneously taken record of a relevant conversation is a relevant fact and is admissible under this section but according to Supreme Court, such evidence must be received with caution.

Mahabir Pd. Verma vs. Surinder Kaur, AIR 1982 SC

The Supreme Court rejected there was no proof of the conversation which it could have been used to corroborate.

R. Donellon

Habit is a best source of opportunity.

Effect is a very relevant fact:

Indian Airlines vs. Madhuri Chaudhary

Inquiry after the happening of event is relevant because it tells about effect.

6. Motive, preparation and previous or subsequent conduct.—(1) Any fact is relevant which shows or constitutes a motive or preparation for any fact in issue or relevant fact.

(2) The conduct of any party, or of any agent to any party, to any suit or proceeding, in reference to such suit or proceeding, or in reference to any fact in issue therein or relevant thereto, and the conduct of any person, an offence against whom is the subject of any proceeding, is relevant, if such conduct influences or is influenced by any fact in issue or relevant fact, and whether it was previous or subsequent thereto.

Explanation 1.-The word "conduct" in this section does not include statements, unless those statements accompany and explain acts other than statements; but this explanation is not to affect the relevancy of statements under any other section of this Adhiniyam.

Explanation 2.— When the conduct of any person is relevant, any statement relevant.

made to him or in his presence and hearing, which affects such conduct, is relevant

ILLUSTRATIONS

(a) A is tried for the murder of B. The facts that A murdered C, that B knew that A had murdered C, and that B had tried to extort money from A by threatening to make his knowledge public, are relevant.

(b) A sues B upon a bond for the payment of money. B denies the making of the bond. The fact that, at the timewhen thebond was alleged to be made, B required money for a particular purpose, is relevant.

(c) A is tried for the murder of B by poison. The fact that, before the death of B, A procured poison similar to that which was administered to B, is relevant.

(d) The question is, whether a certain document is the will of A. The facts that, not long before, the date of the alleged will, A made inquiry into matters to which the provisions of the alleged will relate; that he consulted advocates in reference to making the will, and that he caused drafts of other wills to be prepared, of which he did not approve, are relevant.

(e) A is accused of a crime. The facts that, either before, or at the time of, or after the alleged crime, A provided evidence which would tend to give to the facts of the case an appearance favourable to himself, or that he destroyed or concealed evidence, or prevented the presence or procured the absence of persons who might have been witnesses, or suborned persons to give false evidence respecting it, are relevant.

(f) The question is, whether A robbed B. The facts that, after B was robbed, C said in A's presence "the police are coming to look for the person who robbed B", and that immediately afterwards A ran away, are relevant.

(g) The question is, whether A owes B ten thousand rupees. The facts that A asked C to lend him money, and that D said to C in A's presence and hearing—"I advise you not to trustA,for he owes B ten thousand rupees", and that A went away without making any answer, are relevant facts.

(h) The question is, whether A committed a crime. The fact that A absconded, after receiving a letter, warning A that inquiry was being made for the criminal, and the contents of the letter, are relevant.

(i) A is accused of a crime. The facts that, after the commission of the alleged crime, A absconded, or was in possession of property or the proceeds of property acquired by the crime, or attempted to conceal things which were or might have been used in committing it, are relevant.

(i) The question is, whether A was raped. The fact that, shortly after the alleged rape, A made a complaint relating to the crime, the circumstances under which, and the terms in which, the complaint was made, are relevant. The fact that, without making a complaint, A said that A had been raped is not relevant as conduct under this section, though it may be relevant as a dying declaration under clause (a) of section 26, or as corroborative evidence under section 160.

(k) The question is, whether A was robbed. The fact that, soon after the alleged robbery, A made a complaint relating to the offence, the circumstances under which, and the terms in which, the complaint was made, are relevant. The fact that A said he had been robbed, without making any complaint, is not relevant, as conduct under this section, though it may be relevant as a dying declaration under clause (a) of section 26, or as corroborative evidence under section 160.

Motive

Motive is that which moves a man to do a particular act. Motive in the correct sense is the emotion supposed to have led to the act. It is often proved by the conduct of the accused.

Tara Devi vs. State of UP, AIR 1991 SC

Previous threats, previous altercations, or previous litigations between parties are admitted to show motive. The merely existence of motive is by itself not a incriminating circumstances.

S.C. Bahri vs. State of Bihar, AIR 1994 SC

Sometimes motive plays an important role and becomes a compelling force to commit a crime and, therefore, motive behind the crime is a relevant factor for which evidence may be adduced. But the absence of proof of motive does not render the evidence bearing on the guilt of the accused nonetheless untrustworthy or unreliable because most often it is only the perpetrator of the crime only who knows as to what circumstances promoted him to a certain course of action leading to the commission of the crime.

S. Cr. Mohite vs. State of Maharashtra, AIR 1993 SC

Existence of previous and subsequent similar conduct is relevant to an issue of intention or other state of mind although it cannot be used to prove that the commission of the crime. Evidence of motive becomes important when there is only circumstantial evidence.

Bhagirath vs. State of Haryana, AIR 1996, SC

It was held by the Supreme Court that inadequacy of motive is immaterial where testimony of eye-witness is on the record.

Jarnail Singh vs. State of Haryana, 1993 AIR SC

It was held that where oral or circumstantial evidence adduced had established the charge against the accused, absence of motive would be of no consequence.

Sarojini vs. State of MP, 1993 Cr. L.J. (SC)

It was held that pre-marital demand of dowry and its non-compliance are relevant facts to establish motive.

Preparation

Preparation consists in devising on arranging the means or measures necessary for commission of a crime. Preparation on the part of the accused to accomplish the crime charged, or to prevent its discovery, or to aid his escape, or to avert suspicion from himself are relevant on the question of his guilty.

Conduct

The conduct of any part or his agent in reference to a suit or proceeding will be scanned under this section. A fact can be proved by conduct of a party and by surrounding circumstances, the production of articles by an accused person is relevant as evidence of conduct. Statements accompanying or explaining conduct are also relevant as part of conduct itself.

M. Malkani vs. Maharashtra, AIR 1973 SC

Conversation over telephone for settling details for passing bribe - money was recorded by secret instruments, was held to be evidence of conduct.

Kansa Bahera vs. State of Orissa, AIR 1987 SC

The conduct of being last seen with the deceased is relevant, but not sufficient in itself to support conviction.

Thimma vs. State of Mysore, AIR 1971 SC

The conduct of an accused in absconding when the police get suspicious of his complicity in the offence of murder is relevant under this section and might well be indicative to some extent of guilty mind. But this is not the only conclusion to which it must lead the court. Such is the instinct of self-preservation in an average human being that even innocent persons may, when suspected of grave crimes, be tempted to evade arrest.

7. Facts necessary to explain or introduce fact in issue or relevant facts.—

Facts necessary to explain or introduce a fact in issue or relevant fact, or which support or rebut an inference suggested by a fact in issue or a relevant fact, or which establish the identity of anything, or person whose identity, is relevant

or fix the time or place at which any fact in issue or relevant fact happened, or which show the relation of parties bywhom any such fact was transacted, are relevant in so far as they are necessary for that purpose.

Illustrations

(a) The question is, whether a given document is the will of A. The state of A's property and of his family at the date of the alleged will may be relevant facts.

(b) A sues B for a libel imputing disgraceful conduct to A; B affirms that the matter alleged to be libellous is true. The position and relations of the parties at the time when the libel was published may be relevant facts as introductory to the facts in issue. The particulars of a dispute between A and B about a matter unconnected with the alleged libel are irrelevant, though the fact that there was a dispute may be relevant if it affected the relations between A and B.

(c) A is accused of a crime. The fact that, soon after the commission of the crime, A absconded from his house, is relevant under section 6, as conduct subsequent to and affected by facts in issue. The fact that, at the time when he left home, A had sudden and urgent business at the place to which he went, is relevant, as tending to explain the fact that he left home suddenly. The details of the business on which he left are not relevant, except in so far as they are necessary to show that the business was sudden and urgent.

(d) A sues B for inducing C to break a contract of service made by him with A. C, on leaving A's service, says to A—"I am leaving you because B has made me a better offer". Thisstatement is a relevant fact as explanatory of C's conduct, which is relevant as a fact in issue.

(e) A, accused of theft, is seen to give the stolen property to B, who is seen to give it to A's wife. B says as he delivers it-

-"A says you are to hide this". B's statement is

relevant as explanatory of a fact which is part of the transaction.

(f) A is tried for a riot and is proved to have marched at the head of a mob. The cries of the mob are relevant as explanatory of the nature of the transaction.

COMMENT

The comment mentioned under Section 7 of the Bharatiya Sakshya Adhiniyam, 2023 are based upon Section 9 of the Indian Evidence Act, 1872 (1 of 1872)

Necessity for holding an investigation parade

The necessity for holding an investigation parade can arise only when the accused are not previously known to the witnesses. The whole idea of a test identification parade is that witnesses who claim to have seen the culprits at the time of occurrence are to identify them from the midst of other persons without any aid or any other source.

Udaya Kumar v. State of Tamil Nadu, 2023 INSC 239.

Hardayal vs. UP, AIR 1976 SC

Evidence of other offences committed by the accused is admitted in order to establish his identity or to corroborate the testimony of a witness in a material particular. Identity can also be established by technical evidence like medical report.

Gokaraju Venkatanarasa Raju vs. State of AP, 1993 (SC)

It was held by supreme Court that close relatives of the deceased can identify the decomposed body recovered even after three weeks of the incident.

2. Identification parade

One of the methods of establishing the identity of the accused is "test identification parade"

Its evidence is received under this section. The idea of the parade is to test the veracity of the witness on the question of his capability to identify from among several persons made to stand in a queue, an unknown person whom the witness had seen at the time of the occurrence.

Ashok Narshari Nath vs. State of Maharashtra, 1980 Cr. L.J. (SC)

The witness identified two out of several accused, namely one who assaulted him and one who inflicted fatal injuries on his complainant. It was held by Supreme Court that Test Identification (TI) was good evidence, delay of 44 hours was not so material as to convince the court that the memory of the witness must. have become blurred.

Samappa V. Madar vs. Mysore, AIR 1979 SC

The Supreme Court held that prosecution has to show that the accused was carried for remand ba parda. In absence of it the identification parade will lose its importance.

Weight of identity evidence

The Supreme Court in its decision in Kanta Prasad vs. Delhi

Administration, 1958 SCR, observed that, "the weight to be attached to such identification would be a matter for the court of fact and it is not for the court to reassess the evidence unless exceptional grounds were established necessitating such a course

8. Things said or done by conspirator in reference to common design.-Where there is reasonable ground to believe that two or more persons have conspired together to commit an offence or an actionable wrong, anything said, done or written by any one of such persons in reference to their common intention, after the time when such intention was first entertained by any one of them, is a relevant fact as against each of the persons believed to be so conspiring, as well for the purpose of proving the existence of the conspiracy as for the purpose of showing that any such person was a party to it.

Illustration

Reasonable ground exists for believing that A has joined in a conspiracy to wage war against the State.

The facts that B procured arms in Europe for the purpose of the conspiracy, c collected money in Kolkata for a like object, D persuaded persons to join the conspiracy in Mumbai, E published writings advocating the object in view at Agra, and F transmitted from Delhi to G at Singapore the money which C had collected at Kolkata, and the contents of a letter written by H giving an account of the conspiracy, are each relevant, both to prove the existence of the conspiracy, and to prove A's complicity in it, although he may have been ignorant of all of them, and although the persons by whom they were done were strangers to him, and although they may have taken place before he joined the conspiracy or after he left it.

Bhagwan Swarup vs. State of Maharashtra, AIR 1965 SC –

The expression "in reference to their common intention" in this section is very comprehensive with the result that anything said, done or written by a co-conspirator, after the conspiracy was formed, will be evidence against the other before he entered the field of conspiracy or after he left it. It cannot be used in favour of the other party or for the purpose of the other party or for the purpose of showing that such a person was not a party to the conspiracy.

when a criminal act is done by several persons, in furtherance of the common intention of all, each of such persons is liable for that act in the same manner as if it were done by him alone.

This section makes admissible in evidence things said or done by a conspirator in reference to the common design. It applies to crime as well as torts, i.e. to joint offenders as well as joint tortfeasors. It has no bearing on the question as to how for a conspiracy to commit an offence or actionable wrong is an offence under the Indian Penal Code. It is based upon the principle that, when several persons conspire to commit a crime or a tort, each makes the rest his agent to carry the plan into execution.

Agreement but not direct meeting necessary

Jenkins CJ in Barinder Kumar Ghose vs. Emperor (1909) Calcutta observed

- "Though to establish the charge of conspiracy there must be agreement, there need not be proof of direct meeting or combination, nor need the parties be brought into each other's presence; the agreement may be inferred from circumstances raising a presumption of a common concerted plan to carry out the unlawful design.

So again it is not necessary that all should have joined in the scheme from the first; those who came in at a later stage are equally guilty, provided the agreement be proved.

Kehar Singh vs. Delhi Administration, AIR 1988. SC

The fact that the accused and the person who shot dead the deceased were together at a social gathering sometime before the shooting and isolating themselves at the house top were seen talking and avoided questions as to what they were talking about was held by the Supreme Court to be sufficient to create a reason to believe that they might be conspiring about something. The accused was accordingly sentence to death along with those who actually caused death he was no where there at the place of shooting.

COMMENT

The comment mentioned under Section 8 of the Bharatiya Sakshya Adhiniyam, 2023 are based upon Section 10 of the Indian Evidence Act, 1872 (1 of 1872)

Where prima facie evidence of existence of conspiracy is provided and accepted, the evidence of acts and statements made by any of conspirators in furtherance of common intention is admissible against all. Confession of witnesses recorded long after murder when conspiracy culminated, therefore Section 10, cannot be pressed into service.

Jayendra Saraswathi Swamigal v. State of Tamil Nadu, AIR 2005 SC 716.

9. When facts not otherwise relevant become relevant.-Facts not otherwise relevant are relevant—

(1) if they are inconsistent with any fact in issue or relevant fact;

(2) if by themselves or in connection with other facts they make the existence or non-existence of any fact in issue or relevant fact highly probable or improbable.

Illustrations

i. The question is, whether A committed a crime at Chennai on a certain day. The fact that, on that day, A was at Ladakh is relevant. The fact that, near the time when the crime was committed, A was at a distance from the place where it was committed, which would render it highly improbable, though not impossible, that he committed it, is relevant.

ii. The question is, whether A committed a crime. The circumstances are such that the crime must have been committed either by A, B, C or D. Every fact which shows that the crime could have been committed by no one else, and that it was not committed by either B, C or D, is relevant.

Khaver Sultan vs. Rukha Sultan (1904) Bom LR

The question in issue was whether possession was duly given of certain immovable properties under a deed of gift, so as to make it complete and valid under the Muhammadan Law, it was held that, if the deed of gift must be held to have operated effectually as to immovable property, the fact of this partial delivery, being a collateral fact fulfilling all the requirements of the law, was relevant under this section as making the existence of the facts in issue highly probable.

State of Maharashtra vs. Narsingrao, AIR 1984 SC

The Supreme Court has observed that it is well settled that the plea of alibi (being at another place at the time of commission of crime) must be proved with absolute certainty so as to completely exclude the possibility of the presence of the person concerned at the place of occurrence.

Munir Ad vs. State of Rajasthan, AIR 1989 SC

The presence of the accused at the scene of the crime was established by the FIR, dying declaration and medical evidence, it was held that the plea of alibi raised by the accused was not of any worth.

Pattad Amarappa vs. State of Karnataka, AIR 1989 SC

The plea of alibi could not be sustained owing to uncertainty about the time and place of occurrence.

Gauri Shankar Sharma vs. State of UP, AIR 1990 SC

The Supreme Court cautioned against this that the failure of the accused to establish his presence elsewhere should not be taken to mean inevitably his presence at the spot of the crime or that he was the man behind the murder.

Sakharam vs. State of MP, AIR 1992 SC

The Supreme Court reiterated again that the failure of the accused to substantiate the plea of alibi is not a circumstance which should go against him.

Dudh Nath Pandey v. State of U.P. AIR 1981 SC

Supreme Court stated "The Plea of Alibi postulates the physical impossibility of the presence of the Accused of the Scene of the offence by reason of his presence at another place. The plea can therefore succeed only if it is shown that the Accused was so far away at the relevant time that he could not be present at the place where the crime was committed"

Plea of Alibi must be proved with 'Absolute certainty' so as to completely exclude the possibility of the presence of the person concerned at the place of occurrence:

COMMENT

The comment mentioned under Section 9 of the Bharatiya Sakshya Adhiniyam, 2023 are based upon Section 11 of the Indian Evidence Act, 1872 (1 of 1872)

The victim sustained 100% burn injuries while she was in her matrimonial house at village. The appellant is the wife of the brother of accused no.1. The appellant was living with her husband separately in a different house. Medical certificate is sued by medical superintendent showing accused was admitted in hospital and under went surgery few days before incident and unable to move out of house. The plea of alibi taken by the appellant deserves to be accepted.

Sow. Chhaya v. State of Maharashtra, AIR 2018 SC 3604.

10. Facts tending to enable Court to determine amount are relevant in suits for damages.-In suits in which damages are claimed, any fact which will enable the Court to determine the amount of damages which ought to be awarded, is relevant.

COMMENT

Based on Section 12 Indian Evidence Act . This section enables the court to admit any facts which will help it to determine the amount of damages which ought to be awarded to a party when damages are claimed in a suit, the amount of damages is a fact in issue.

"Damages" are the pecuniary satisfaction which the plaintiff may obtain by success in an action. They are limited to the loss which the plaintiff has actually sustained.

11. Facts relevant when right or custom is in question.-Where the question is as to the existence of any right or custom, the following facts are relevant-

(a) any transaction by which the right or custom in question was created, claimed, modified, recognised, asserted or denied, or which was inconsistent with its existence;

(b) particular instances in which the right or custom was claimed, recognised or exercised, or in which its exercise was disputed, asserted or departed from.

Illustration

The question is, whether A has a right to a fishery. A deed conferring the fishery on A's ancestors, a mortgage of the fishery by A's father, a subsequent grant of the fishery by A's father, irreconcilable with the mortgage, particular instances in which A's father exercised the right, or in which the exercise of the right was stopped by A's neighbours, are relevant facts.

Right

The term "right" comprehends every right known to the law. It includes both corporeal and incorporeal rights including "a right of ownership".

The **Collector of Gorakhpur vs. Palakdhari Singh (1889) (All) FB** - This section is not confined to public rights only but it covers private rights also.

Custom

A custom is a rule which in a particular family or in a particular district has from long usage obtained the force of law. The English rule that "a custom, in order that it may be legal and binding must have been used so long that the memory of man runneth not to the contrary" does not apply to conditions in India.

A custom observed in a particular district derives its force from the fact that it has, from long usage, obtained in that district the force of law.

A custom to be recognised by a court must fulfil following eight requirements:-

i) Ancient

ii) Continuous and uniform

iii) Reasonable

iv) Certain

v) Compulsory and not optional

vi) Peaceful observation

vii) Not immoral

viii) Conformity with law.

A custom may be general, public or private.

In order to prove a custom -

a) The evidence should be such as to prove the uniformity and continuity of the usage and the conviction of those following it that they were acting in accordance with law.

b)Evidence of acts of the kind, acquiescence in those acts, their publicity decisions of courts or even of panchayats upholding such acts, the statements of experienced and competent persons of their belief that such acts were legal and valid will all be admissible but actual examples of the usage asserted must be shown.

A trade usage or custom may be proved in the same way as a family custom.

(Rajendra Ram vs. Devendra Das, AIR 1973 SC)

Saraswati Ammal vs. Jagadambal, AIR 1973 SC

It is incumbent on a party setting up a custom to allege and prove the custom on which he relies and it is not any theory of custom or deductions from other customs which can be made a rule of decisions.

Rajendra Ram vs. Devendra Das, AIR 1973 SC

The rule of custom should prevail in all cases on if any aberration have to be corrected such correction must take the court in the direction of re-establishing the rule of custom.

Transaction

A transaction, in the ordinary sense of the word, is some business or dealing which is carried on or transacted between two or more persons.

Gajanfar Ali Khan v. Province of Assam, (1944) 1 Calcutta

It was held that Judgments not inter partes might be admissible in evidence as establishing a particular transaction, if any, by which the relevant right was asserted, recognised, claimed or denied, but in no case the reasons and findings of fact arrived at in them would be admissible in evidence.

Gopika Raman Roy v. Atal Singh (1929) 1A, Privy Council

A finding of fact arrived at on the evidence in one case is not evidence of that fact in another case between different parties.

Rama Chandra v. Gadhadhar Mohapatra, AIR 1980 Orissa

It may be taken to be fairly settled that the judgment in a previous suit though not inter partes is admissible in proof of a transaction or a particular instance in which the relationship was asserted and recognised or denied. A previous judgment though not conclusive proof is admissible in evidence like any other fact to be weighed in the balance. It is not the correctness of the previous decision but the fact that there has been a previous decision that is established by the judgment.

COMMENT

Based on Section 13 of Indian Evidence Act .The cases this section is intended to meet are those in which the right or custom in question is regarded as capable of surviving repeated instances of its assertion and denial.

12. Facts showing existence of state of mind, or of body or bodily feeling.—

Facts showing the existence of any state of mind, such as intention, knowledge, good faith, negligence, rashness, ill-will or goodwill towards any particular person, or showing the existence of any state of body or bodily feeling, are relevant, when the existence of any such state of mind or body or bodily feeling is in issue or relevant.

Explanation 1.— A fact relevant as showing the existence of a relevant state of mind must show that the state of mind exists, not generally, but in reference to the particular matter in question.

Explanation 2.-But where, upon the trial of a person accused of an offence, the previous commission by the accused of an offence is relevant within the meaning of this section, the previous conviction of such person shall also be a relevant fact.

Illustrations

(a) A is accused of receiving stolen goods knowing them to be stolen. It is proved that he was in possession of a particular stolen article. The fact that, at the same time, he was in possession of many other stolen articles is relevant, as tending to show that he knew each and all of the articles of which he was in possession to be stolen.

(b) A is accused of fraudulently delivering to another person a counterfeit currency Which, at the time when he delivered it, he knew to be counterfeit. The fact that, at the time of its delivery, A was possessed of a number of other pieces of counterfeit currency . is relevant. The fact that A had been previously convicted of delivering to another person as genuine a counterfeit currency knowing it to be counterfeit is relevant.

to B, are relevant.

(d) The question is, whether A, the acceptor of a bill of exchange, knew that the name of the payee was fictitious. The fact that A had accepted other bills drawn in the same manner before they could have been transmitted to him by the payee if the payee had been a real person, is relevant, as showing that A knew that the payee was a fictitious person.

(e) A is accused of defaming B by publishing an imputation intended to harm the reputation of B. The fact of previous publications by A respecting B, showing ill-will on the part of A towards B is relevant, as proving A's intention to harm B's reputation by the particular publication in question. The facts that there was no previous quarrel between A and B, and that A repeated the matter complained of as he heard it, are relevant, as showing that A did not intend to harm the reputation of B.

(f) A is sued by B for fraudulently representing to B that C was solvent, whereby B, being induced to trust C, who was insolvent, suffered loss. The fact that, at the time when A represented C to be solvent, C was supposed to be solvent by his neighbours and by persons dealing with him, is relevant, as showing that A made the representation in good faith.

(g) A is sued by B for the price of work done by B, upon a house of which A is owner, by the order of C, a contractor. A's defence is that B's contract was with C. The fact that A paid C for the work in question is relevant, as proving that A did, in good faith, make over to C the management of the work in question, so that C was in a position to contract with B on C's own account, and not as agent for A.

(h) A is accused of the dishonest misappropriation of property which he had found, and the question is whether, when he appropriated it, he believed in good faith that the real owner could not be found. The fact that public notice of the loss of the property had been given in the place where A was, is relevant, as showing that A did not in good faith believe that the real owner of the property could not be found. The fact that A knew, or had reason to believe, that the notice was given fraudulently by C, who had heard of the loss of the property and wished to set up a false claim to it, is relevant, as showing that the fact that A knew of the notice did not disprove A's good faith.

(i) A is charged with shooting at B with intent to kill him. In order to show As intent, the fact of A's having previously shot at B may be proved.

(i) A is charged with sending threatening letters to B. Threatening letters previously sent by A to B may be proved, as showing the intention of the letters.

(K) The question is, whether A has been guilty of cruelty towards B, his wife.

Expressions of their feeling towards each other shortly before or after the alleged cruelty are relevant facts.

(.) The question is, whether A's death was caused by poison. Statements made by A during his illness as to his symptoms are relevant facts.

(m) The question is, what was the state of A's health at the time when an assurance on his life was effected. Statements made by A as to the state of his health at or near the time in question are relevant facts.

(n) A sues B for negligence in providing him with a car for hire not reasonably fit for use, whereby A was injured. The fact that B's attention was drawn on other occasions to the defect of that particular car is relevant. The fact that B was habitually negligent about the cars which he let to hire is irrelevant.

(0) A is tried for the murder of B by intentionally shooting him dead. The fact that A on other occasions shot at B is relevant as showing his intention to shoot B.

The fact that A was in the habit of shooting at people with intent to murder them is irrelevant.

(P) A is tried for a crime. The fact that he said something indicating an intention to commit that particular crime is relevant. The fact that he said something indicating a general disposition to commit crimes of that class is irrelevant.

Ingredients

the fact showing the existence of any sale of -

a) Mind (e.g. intention, knowledge, good faith, negligence, rashness, ill-will, good will) or

b) Body

c) Bodily feelings when such state of mind or body is relevant are relevant facts and evidence can be given in legal proceedings.

- Intention, knowledge and similar other states of mind, are matters of cogent inquiry in criminal cases; in some civil cases they are very material, e.g., some civil cases they are very material, e.g., in cases of malicious prosecution, fraud, negligence etc.

Specific state of mind, not general (Explanation 1)

Under this Explanation evidence of general reputation is excluded. The evidence relating to the state of mind of a person must show that the state of mind exists that generally but in reference to the particular matter in question. Evidence of general disposition, habit or tendencies is inadmissible. Anything having a distinct and immediate reference to the particular matter in question is admissible.

Previous conviction (Explanation 2)

This Explanation distinctly states that, where the previous commission of an offence is relevant, the previous conviction of such person should also be a relevant fact. Previous conviction became relevant when the existence of any state of mind, or body, or bodily feeling, is in issue, are relevant **[Emperor v. Allo Miya Husan, (1903) Bom LR].**

- The previous conviction is nothing more than evidence of bad character which is Excluded. This Section does not extend to cases where the question of guilt or innocence depends upon actual facts and not upon the state of a man's mind or feeling.

COMMENT

Based on section 14 of Indian Evidence Act . Phipson has stated, "The principle on which evidence of similar acts is admissible is not to show that because the defendant has committed one crime. Therefore , he would likely to commit another , but to establish the onimus of the act and to rebut , by anticipation , the obvious defences ,of ignorance, accident , mistake or other innocent state of mind."

The conduct of each individual co-conspirator including his acts, writing and Statements irrespective of the time to which it relates can be relied on by the prosecution to show the criminality of the intention of the individual accused with reference to his proved participation in the alleged conspiracy to rebut a probable defence that the participation, though proved, was innocent. Such evidence is admissible under this section. **[Sardul Singh Coveeshar vs. State of Bombay,**

(1958) SCR 161]

13. Facts bearing on question whether act was accidental or intentional.—

When there is a question whether an act was accidental or intentional, or done with a particular knowledge or intention, the fact that such act formed part of a series of similar occurrences, in each of which the person doing the act was concerned, is relevant.

Illustrations

(a) A is accused of burning down his house in order to obtain money for which it is insured. The facts that A lived in several houses successively each of which he insured, in each of which a fire occurred, and after each of which fires A received payment from a different insurance company, are relevant, as tending to show that the fires were not accidental.

(b) A is employed to receive money from the debtors of B. It is A's duty to make entries in a book showing the amounts received by him. He makes an entry showing that on a particular occasion he received less than he really did receive. The question is, whether this false entry was accidental or intentional. The facts that other entries made by A in the same book are false, and that the false entry is in each case in favour of A, are relevant.

(c) A is accused of fraudulently delivering to B a counterfeit currency. The question is, whether the delivery of the currency was accidental. The facts that, soon before or soon after the delivery to B, A delivered counterfeit currency to C, D and E are relevant, as showing that the delivery to B was not accidental.

Ingredients

i. The question is whether an act was (i) accidental or (ii) intentional.

i. The fact that it formed part of a series of similar occurrences.
ii. Is relevant to show that the act was not, accidental but it was intentional.

Principle

Where it is uncertain, whether an act was done with a guilty knowledge or intention or whether it was innocent or accidental, proof that it formed one of a series of similar acts raises the presumption that the act in question and the others, together forming a series, were done upon system, and were therefore not innocent or accidental.

Needle Industries (India) Ltd. v. Needle Industries Newly (India) Ltd. AIR 1981 SC

It was not shown that the director of a company was instrumental in the late posting of the notice of a shareholders' meeting, this section was not attracted.

There was no question of the delay being intentional or accidental.

Comparison of Section 12 and 13

Section 12 provides that facts showing the existence of any state of mind, such as intention or knowledge, are relevant, when the existence of any such state of mind is in issue or relevant; and Section 13 provides specially for allowing evidence of similar occurrences, in each of which the person doing the act was concerned, whenever there is a question whether an act is done with a particular knowledge or intention.

Amrit Lal Hazara vs. Emperor (1915) Calcutta

Evidence tending to show that the accused has been guilty of criminal acts other than those covered by the indictment is not admissible unless upon the issue whether the acts charged against the accused were designed or accidental, or unless to rebut a defence otherwise open to him.

COMMENT

The comment mentioned under Section 13 of the Bharatiya Sakshya Adhiniyam, 2023 are based upon Section 15 of the Indian Evidence Act, 1872 (1 of 1872)

Notwithstanding is the Act, but subject to the provision of this section, a confession made by a person before a police officer not lower is rank, than a superintendent of police and recorded by such police officer either in writing or on any mechanical device like cassettes, tapes or sound tracks from out of which sounds or images can be reproduced, shall be admissible in the trial of such person or co-accused, abettor or conspirator for an offence under this act.

State of Maharashtra v. Kamal Ahmed Mohammed Vakil Ansari, 2013 Cri.L.).

14. Existence of course of business when relevant.—When there is a question whether a particular act was done, the existence of any course of business, according to which it naturally would have been done, is a relevant fact.

Illustrations

(a) The question is, whether a particular letter was dispatched. The facts that it was the ordinary course of business for all letters put in a certain place to be carried to the post, and that particular letter was put in that place are relevant.

(b) The question is, whether a particular letter reached A. The facts that it was posted in due course, and was not returned through the Return Letter Office, are relevant.

Ingredients

i) When there is a question whether a particular act is done or not.

ii) The existence of any course of business, according to which it naturally would have been done.

iii) It will be presumed that the act was done.

iv)The burden of proof that the act is not done is upon the party who alleges it.

Omnia proesumuntur rite esse acta

It means all acts are presumed to be rightly done. Section 16 of the Evidence Act is based upon the above mentioned maxim. This maxim is based on the fact that the conduct of men in official and commercial matters is, to a great extent, uniform. In such cases, there is a strong presumption that the general regularity will not, in any particular instance, be departed from. This is a rebuttable presumption.

Mubarak Ali Ahmed v. State of Bombay, AIR 1957 SC

It was held by the Supreme Court that this section covers both private and public offices. The usage in a private house, however methodical/ cannot convey the same weight as the ordinary routine of an office.

Computer hearsay

A great deal of information is now-a-days stored in and dispensed by computers. The effect of hearsay rule on the admissibility of such information was considered in R v. Ewing (1983) All ER. It was held that the print-out was relevant because it is a document which was or formed part of a record relating to any trade or business.

COMMENT

Based on Section 16 of Indian Evidence Act . Under this section , when the ordinary course of a particular business is proved , the court is asked to presume that , on the particular occasion in question , there was no departure from the ordinary and general rule.

Admissions

15. Admission defined.-An admission is a statement, oral or documentary or contained in electronic form, which suggests any inference as to any fact in issue or relevant fact, and which is made by any of the persons, and under the circumstances, hereinafter mentioned.

TYPES OF ADMISSIONS

1. **JUDICIAL / FORMAL ADMISSION :-** formal admission are judicial admission and in such a case there is no need to prove the facts admitted. This is made before court of law and is made by party during proceedings of the case .
2. **INFORMAL / CASUAL ADMISSION :-** Informal Admission are usually made in casual conversation in ignorance of the possibility of it being used in future litigation .

for eg :- with family , friends neighbour and so on. It is made outside the court of law in ordinary court of life.

Admission those are informal in nature and do not appear on the record of the case are referred to as informal or casual admission .

3. **Admission by Conduct :-** Those which are made by conduct for eg:- if person during informal interrogation ran away from that place this conduct of the person is said to be Admission by Conduct .

NOTE :- SILENCE IS ALSO ADMISSION BY CONDUCT SILENCE WILL AMOUNT TO ADMISSION ONLY IF IT IS NATURAL TO EXPECT A DENIAL OR REPLY.

Ingredients

(i)An admission is a statement (i) oral or (ii) documentary requires State to a particular person.

Bhogilal vs. State SC - Statement means something stated. it does not require state to a particular person.

(ii)Which suggests any inference as to any (i) fact in issue or (ii) relevant fact

iv. Which is made by a person authorised by the Bhartiyan Sakshya Adhiniyam
v. And under the circumstances as described by the Bhartiyan Sakshya Adhiniyam

COMMENT

Based on section 17 of Indian Evidence Act .An "admission" is a statement of fact which waives or dispenses with the production of evidence by conceding that the fact asserted by the opponent is

true.

Thiru John vs. Returning Officer, AIR 1977 SC

The Supreme Court has observed: Admissions are defined in Sections 17 and 20 and fulfilling the requirements of Section21 are substantive evidence, prapio vigare. An admission is the best evidence against the party making it and, though not conclusive, shifts the onus to the maker on the principle that what a party himself admits to be true may be reasonably presumed to be true so that until the presumption is rebutted the fact admitted must be taken to be true.

Mohammad Koya vs. Muthubona (1979) SCR

The Supreme Court observed that an admission must be examined as a whole and not in parts.

Union of India vs. Haksh Builders etc., AIR 1977 SC

The Supreme Court cited a statement from its own earlier decision to the effect that an admission is substantive evidence of the fact admitted and when properly proved is relevant irrespective of the fact that the maker approved in the witness-box or not and when he appears, whether he was confronted with those statements or not in case he made a statement contrary to his admissions.

Banarsi Das vs. Kanshi Ram, AIR 1963 SC

The SC observed that admission are weak kind of evidence and the court may reject them if they are untrue

An admission in so far as facts are concerned would bind the maker of the admission but not in so far as it relates to a question of law.

In English Law, the term "admission" is used in civil cases; whereas the term

"confession" is used in criminal cases as acknowledgement of guilt.

Rakesh Wadhwa vs J.I Corporation

The S.C held that admission are not conclusive proof of the matter admitted unless they operate as Estoppels. Therefore the value of evidence depends upon thecircumstances under which they are made and also by whom it is made .

RULES OF ADMISSION

1. Admission is substantive piece of evidence against person making it.
2. Admission must be made expressly and not impliedly
3. Admission must be made voluntarily.
4. It can be in form of judicial and Extrajudicial .
5. Admission made voluntary before judicial or quasi- judicial authority and statement not retracted before being acted upon by the other party , then it also act as estoppel on the person making it.

EVIDENTIARY VALUE OF ADMISSION

COURT IN THE CASE OF NAGINDAS RAMDAS VS DALPATRAM ICCHARAM OBSERVED THAT JUDICIAL ADMISSION MADE DURING THE COURSE OF PROCEEDING BY THE PARTIES OR AGENT IS STRONGER EVIDENCE THAN INFORMAL ADMISSION MADE OUTSIDE THE COURT.

SECTION 25 OF BHARTIYAN SAKSHYA ADHINIYAM deals with the effect of admission and stipulates about the evidentiary value of admissions. All that this Section provides is that an admission, unless it operates as an estoppel, is not conclusive.

Section 25 OFBHARTIYAN SAKSHYA ADHINIYAM

This Section states that the admissions are not conclusive proof of the matters admitted but they may operate as estoppels under this Act.

Admissions are not conclusive of the matter admitted that is although they are good evidence against the party making them or his representative in interest, he is not bound by them and is at liberty to prove that they were made under a mistake of law or fact, or were untrue or were made under threat, inducement or fraud unless they operate as estoppels.

Admissions are Substantive Evidence

Section 25 says that admission is not conclusive proof, but it does not say that an admission is not sufficient proof without corroboration.

They are strong pieces of evidence against a party making it unless they are proved to be false.

Thus, if the admissions are not explained by the person by whom it is made, it is a very strong piece of evidence against the maker.

Principles Underlying Section 25

The principles underlying the evidentiary value of an admission under Section 25may be summarized as:

An admission constitutes a substantive piece of evidence as it can be relied upon for proving the truth of the facts incorporated therein.

An admission has the effect of shifting the onus of proving to the contrary on the party against whom it is produced with the result that it casts an imperative duty on such party to explain it. In the absence of satisfactory explanation, it is presumed to be true.

An admission in order to be competent and to have the value and effect referred to above should be clear, certain and definite and not ambiguous or confused.

Admissions as Estoppels

Where an admission operates as an estoppel, the party admitting the fact will not be allowed to go against the facts admitted.

Admissions which have been acted upon by others are conclusive against the party making it.

Estoppel is a conclusive admission.

Admission as waiver of proof / Fact Admitted need not be proved (section 53)

If the party has admitted the fact , it dispenses when the necessity of proving that fact against him

After analysing section 53 and section 25 of this Act we conclude that according to section 25 admission are not conclusive proof of fact admitted , it is only a prima facie proof of the fact . thus admission is substantive admission of fact admitted and if duly proved it continues a good evidence

According to section 53 facts admitted in proceeding by the parties does not require any proof that is waiver of proof .

Effect of admission:

1. Admission act as a waiver of proof - if party has admitted a fact, it dispenses with the necessity of proving that fact against him.

2 Admission is a substantive piece of evidence.

3- Admission is not a conclusive proof A person who has admitted the fact has right to contradict it in subsequent proceeding. Therefore, he can rebut it by saying that it was given voluntarily under stress etc.

4. Admission may operate as estoppel

Difference between Admission and Confession

CONFESSION ADMISSION

1. A confession is a 1- while an admission usually

statement made by a relates to a civil transaction
accused person which and compromises all
is sought to be proved statements amounting
against him in criminal to admission.
proceedings to establish
the commission of an
offence by him.

2. A confession if 2- whereas an admission is

deliberately and not a conclusive proof of
Voluntary made may matters admitted , but
be accepted as conclusive operate as an estoppel
in itself of the matters
confessed.

3. A confession always goes 3- An admission may be used

against the person on behalf of the person
making it making it under exception

4. The confession of one of provided in section 19.

Two or more accused 4- but an admission by one
Jointly tried for the same of several defendants in a
Offence can be taken suit is no evidence against
Into consideration against against another defendant.
The co accused 5- statement is a genus

5. Statement is a genus and and admission is the

Confession is the sub- species
species

16. Admission by party to proceeding or his agent.—(1) Statements made by a party to the proceeding, or by an agent to any such party, whom the Court regards, under the circumstances of the case, as expressly or impliedly authorised by him to make them, are admissions.

(2) Statements made by—

(i) parties to suits suing or sued in a representative character, are not admissions, unless they were made while the party making them held that character; or

(ii) (a) persons who have any proprietary or pecuniary interest in the subject matter of the proceeding, and who make the statement in their character of persons so interested; or

(b) persons from whom the parties to the suit have derived their interest in the subject matter of the suit,

are admissions, if they are made during the continuance of the interest of the persons making the statements.

Ingredients

Section 16 lays down fine classes of persons who can make an admission -

a) Party to the proceeding.

b) Agent authorised by such party.

C) Party suing or sued in a representative character making admissions while holding such character.

d) Persons who have any proprietary or pecuniary interest in the subject-matter of the proceeding during the continuance of such interest.

e) Person from who the parties to the suit have derived their interest in the subject-matter of the suit during the continuance of such interest.

Party to the proceedings

What is admitted by a party to be true must be presumed to be true unless the contrary is shown.

Nagubai vs. B. Shama Rao, AIR 1956 SC

But before it should be relied upon it must be shown that there was a clear and unambiguous statement made by a party such as will be conclusive unless explained.

Agent

The admissions of an agent are admissible because the principle is bound by the acts of his agent done in the course of business and within the scope of his authority.

Sri Chand Gupta vs. Gulzar Singh, AIR 1992 SC

The Apex Court held that before the statement of an agent can be relevant as admissions, the fact of agency must be proud

- Admissions of facts made by a pleader in the conduct of a suit on his clients behalf are binding on the client. But a party is not bound by a pleader's admission in argument on what is a pure question of law.

An admission by a counsel or a pleader on a point of law cannot bind the client.

Raghunath vs. State of UP, AIR 1973 SC

The testimony of counsel that the thumb impression taken as a specimen was that of his client cannot be excluded on the ground that a counsel cannot admit facts on client's behalf.

- An admission or a confession of judgment by one of several defendants in a suit in no evidence against another defendant. No defendant can, by an admission or consent, convey the right, or delegate the authority to one, for more than his own share in property.

Raj Kumar vs. Official Receiver, M/S Chiranji Lal Ram Chand, AIR 1996 SC

Admission by one of the co-owners that the other co-owner had one-third
share in the joint properties, can be relied upon.

- Partners are agents of one another so far as the business of partnership is concerned. So, an admission of a partner can be relied upon.

- The admissions of a guardian ad litem, or next friend, do not bind the minor. The guardian of an infant has no power to bind him by admissions.

Annapagauda vs. Sangadyapa (1901) Bom LR

The Bombay High Court is of the view that a guardian appointed under the Guardians and Wards Act can sign an acknowledgement of liability in respect of, or pay in part the principal of a debt, so as to extend the period of limitation against his ward, provided the guardian's act was for the benefit of the ward's property.

Party suing or sued in a representative character

This means trustees, executors, administrators, managers in the character of an executor or administrator; or the assignee of a bankrupt. It is important that such persons must make "the statement in their character of persons so interested."

Person who has any proprietary or pecuniary interest

An admission by a party is not possible after parting with his interest in the property. An admission made by one of several parties in fraud of the others jointly interests will not bind the others. **[Srichand Gupta vs. Gulzar Singh, AIR**

1999 SC]

Persons from whom the parties to the suit have derived their interest in the subject-matter of the suit

Statements made either by the parties interested or by persons whom the parties to the suit have derived their interest are admissions only if they are made during the continuance of the interest of the persons making the statement.

This clause indicates that there ought to be a privity, i.e. mutual or successive relationship to the same right of property. Privies are of three kinds:

i) Privies in blood, as an heir, an ancestor and coparceners.

ii) Privies in law, as executor and testator, administrator and a person dying intestate.

ii. Privies in estate or interest, as vendor and purchaser, lessor and lessee, mortgagor and mortgagee, donor and donee.

Comment :- Based upon Section 18 of Indian Evidence Act.

17. Admissions by persons whose position must be proved as against party to suit.-Statements made by persons whose position or liability, it is necessary to prove as against any party to the suit, are admissions, if such statements would be relevant as against such persons in relation to such position or liability in a suit brought by or against them, and if they are made Whilst the person making them occupies such position or is subject to such liability.

Illustration

A undertakes to collect rents for B. B sues A for not collecting rent due from C to B. A denies that rent was due from C to B. A statement by C that he owed B rent is anadmission, and is a relevant fact as against A, if A denies that C did owe rent to B.

Ingredients

a) Statements made by persons

b) Whose position or liability it is necessary to prove as against any party to the suit, are admissions,

c) If such statements would be relevant as against such persons in relation to such position or liability in a suit brought by or against them,

d) And if they are made whilst the person making them occupies such position or is subject to such liability.

Object

The object of this Section is not to lay down that certain statements are relevant or admissible but merely to add to the category of persons by whom a statement may be made before it can be considered to an admission within the terms of the Act.

Principle

This Section forms an exception to the rule that statements made by strangers to a proceeding are not admissible as against the parties.

Laxmi Bai vs. A. Chandravati, AIR 1995, Orissa

Execution of a will cannot be doubted merely because of delay in applying for letters of administration which was satisfactorily explained, more so when due execution of the will was admitted by preferential heirs to the estate of the testoree against their own interest.

Comment:- based on section 19 of Indian Evidence Act.

18. Admissions by persons expressly referred to by party to suit.-Statements made by persons to whom a party to the suit has expressly referred for information in reference to a matter in dispute are admissions.

Illustrations

The question is, whether a horse sold by A to B is sound.

A says to B-"Go and ask C, C knows all about it". C’s statement is an admission.

Ingredients

a) Out of two parties to a suit, one party

b) Refers third person for information

c) In reference to a matter in dispute

d) The third person makes a statement in respect of property or matter in dispute

e) The statement of third person is relevant and an admission

Comment

Based on Section 20 of Indian Evidence Act

This Section forms another exception to the rule that admissions by strangers to a suit are not relevant.

19. Proof of admissions against persons making them, and by or on their behalf.-Admissions are relevant and may be proved as against the person who makes them, or his representative in interest; but they cannot be proved by or on behalf of the person who makes them or by his representative in interest, except in the following cases, namely:—

(i) An admission may be proved by or on behalf of the person making it, when it is of such a nature that, if the person making it were dead, it would be relevant as between third persons under section 26;

(ii) An admission may be proved by or on behalf of the person making it, when it consists of a statement of the existence of any state of mind or body, relevant or in issue, made at or about the time when such state of mind or body existed, and is accompanied by conduct rendering its falsehood improbable;

(iii) an admission may be proved by or on behalf of the person making it, if it is relevant otherwise than as an admission.

Illustrations

(a) The question between A and B is, whether a certain deed is or is not forged.

A affirms that it is genuine, B that it is forged. A may prove a statement by B that the deed is genuine, and B may prove a statement by A that deed is forged; but A cannot prove a statement by himself that the deed is genuine, nor can B prove a statement by himself that the deed is forged.

(b) A, the captain of a ship, is tried for casting her away. Evidence is given to show that the ship was taken out of her proper course. A produces a book kept by him in the ordinary course of his business showing observations alleged to have been taken by him from day to day, and indicating that the ship was not taken out of her proper course. A may prove these statements, because they would be admissible between third parties, if he were dead, under clause (b) of section 26.

(c) A is accused of a crime committed by him at Kolkata. He produces a letter written by himself and dated at Chennai on that day, and bearing the Chennai post-mark of that day. The statement in the date of the letter is admissible, because, if A were dead, it would be admissible under clause (b) of section 26.

(d) A is accused of receiving stolen goods knowing them to be stolen. He offers to prove that he refused to sell them below their value. A may prove these statements, thoughthey areadmissions, because they are explanatory of conduct influenced by facts in issue.

e) A is accused of fraudulently having in his possession counterfeit coin which he knew to be counterfeit he offers to prove that he asked a skillful person to examine the currency as he doubted whether it was counterfeit or not, and that person did examine it and told him it was genuine. A may prove these facts for the reasons stated in the last preceding illustration.

Ingredients

a) An admission is relevant and may be proved as against (i) the person who makes it or ii) his representative in interest.

b) It cannot be proved by or on behalf of the person who makes it or by his representatives

c) Except in three cases -

i) When it is of such a nature that, if the person making it were dead, it would be relevant as between third person under Section 26;

ii) When it consists of a statement of the existence of any state of mind or body made at or about the time when such state of mind or body existed and is accompanied by conduct rendering its falsehood improbable;

iii. If it is relevant otherwise than as an admission.

Comment

Based on Section 21 of Indian Evidence Act . This section lays down as a general rule that admissions are relevant and may be proved against the person who makes them or his representative in interest.

Admission duly proved are admissible evidence irrespective of whether the party making them appeared in the witness-box or not and whether that party when appearing as witness was confronted with those statements in case he made a statement contrary to those admission. **[Bharat Singh vs. Bhagirathi, AIR 1966 SC]**

K.S. Srinivasan vs. Union of India, AIR 1958 SC

The effect usually given to admissions proved true or not, does not matter. The effective point is that they destroy the force of inconsistent statements made later. They may operate as an estoppel.

Mahendra vs. Sushila, AIR 1965 SC

An erroneous admission does not bind the person making such admission. Admission must be considered as a whole but the court is not bound to believe or disbelieve the statement as a whole.

Basant Singh vs. Janki Singh, AIR 1967 SC

An admission made by a party in a plaint signed and verified by him may be used against him in other suits. In other suits, this admission cannot be regarded as conclusive, and it is open to the party to show that it is not true.

Biswanath Pd. vs. Dwarka Pd., AIR 1974 SC

An admission is distinct from the former statement of a witness which is cited to contradict him. An admission can be proved without confronting the maker with his earlier statements.

Exceptions

Admissions cannot be proved by or on behalf of the person who makes them, or by his representative in interest , except

a) When it is of such a nature that, if the person making it were dead, it would be relevant as between third persons under Section 26;

b) When it consists of a statement of the existence of any state of mind or body at or about the time when such state of mind or body existed, and is accompanied by conduct rendering its falsehood improbable.

c) When it is relevant otherwise than as an admission.

Basanti vs. State of HP, 1987 Cr.L.J. (SC)

The statement outside the court by the wife of the deceased that she and other named person had committed the murder was held to be not provable under this section.

Bhim Singh v. Kan Singh 1980 SC

In this case the dispute was about the ownership of some property. The legal heirs were claiming it from the person in whose name their deceased father had brought the property. A witness appeared to tell to the court that while the deceased was talking with him, he said that he had brought the property in the other person's name with a view to making him the owner and that he intended to settle more property on him. The statement was held to be relevant being made by the maker against his proprietary interest.

Comment:- Based on section 21 of Indian Evidence Act

20. When oral admissions as to contents of documents are relevant.-Oral admissions as to the contents of a document are not relevant, unless and until the party proposing to prove them shows that he is entitled to give secondary evidence of the contents of such document under the rules hereinafter contained, or unless the genuineness of a document produced is in question.

Ingredients

Oral admissions as to the contents of a document are not relevant unless

a) The party proposing to prove them shows that he is entitled to give secondary evidence of the contents of such documents, or

b)The genuineness of the document produced is in question.

Comment:- Based on Section 22 of Indian Evidence Act.

21. Admissions in civil cases when relevant.-In civil cases no admission is relevant, if it is made either upon an express condition that evidence of it is not to be given, or under circumstances from which the Court can infer that the parties agreed together that evidence of it should not be given.

Explanation.-Nothing in this section shall be taken to exempt any advocate from giving evidence of any matter of which he may be compelled to give evidence under sub-sections (1) and (2) of section 132.

Ingredients

An admission is not relevant in a civil case if it is made.

a) Upon an express condition that evidence of itis not to be given, or

b) Under circumstances from which the court can infer that the parties agreed together that evidence of it should be given.

Comment

Based on section 23 of Indian Evidence Act . This section gives effect to the maxim "interest rei publicae ut sit finis litium (it is for the interest of the state that there should be an end of litigation).

- This section protects communications made "without prejudice" confidential overtures of pacification and any other offers or propositions between litigating parties, expressly or impliedly made without prejudice are excluded on grounds of public policy.

Without Prejudice

In re River Steamer Company (1871) LR

It was held that - The expression 'without prejudice' means without prejudice to the writer of the letter if the terms he proposes are not accepted. It means this, "I make you an offer which you may accept or not as you like; but if you do not accept it, my having made it is to have no effect at all'.

The Lucknow Improvement Trust vs. P.L. Jaitley & Co. (1929) Luck

If the letter marked "without prejudice" is tendered in evidence and the other party admits them, the admission implies that the privilege is withdrawn and the letters are free to be used as evidence in a judicial proceeding.

Letters so marked show the writer's desire as to the privilege, but unless there are circumstances from which it can be inferred that the other party agreed to respect the privileges, the letter cannot be excluded under this section.

- The reply to a letter written "without prejudice" cannot be admitted in evidence even though not guarded in a similarmanner. The words once used will exclude an entire correspondence.

- An admission made to a stranger, under whatever terms as to secrecy, is not protected by law from disclosure.

- Under Explanation to Section 23, the legal advisor of the party will not be prevented from giving evidence of any communication made in furtherance of any illegal purpose or any fact showing that crime or fraud has been committed since his employment.

Nagindas Ramdas v. Dalpatram Ichharam 1974 SC

It was held that "Admission in a pleading or judicial admissions, admissible under section 58 of the Evidence Act, made by parties or their agent at or before the hearing of the case, stand on a higher footing than evidentiary admissions.

22. Confession caused by inducement, threat, coercion or promise, when irrelevant in criminal proceeding.—A confession made by an accused person is irrelevant in a criminal proceeding, if the making of the confession appears to the Court to have been caused by any inducement, threat, coercion or promise having reference to the charge against the accused person, proceeding from a person in authority and sufficient, in the opinion of the Court, to give the accused person grounds which would appear to him reasonable for supposing that by making it he would gain any advantage or avoid any evil of a temporal nature in reference to the proceedings against him:

Provided that if the confession is made after the impression caused by any such inducement, threat, coercion or promise has, in the opinion of the Court, been fully removed, it is relevant:

Provided further that if such a confession is otherwise relevant, it does not become irrelevant merely because it was made under a promise of secrecy, or in consequence of a deception practised on the accused person for the purpose of obtaining it, or when he was drunk, or because it was made in answer to questions which he need not have answered, whatever may have been the form of those questions, or because he was not warned that he was not bound to make such confession, and that evidence of it might be given against him.

Ingredients

A "confession", in an admission made at any time by any person charged with a crime stating stating or suggesting an inference that he committed the crime

a) if it is obtained by any (i) inducement, (ii) threat, (iii promise;

b) Such inducement etc. must have reference to the charge;

c) Such inducement, etc. must proceed from a person in authority:

Such inducement etc. must be sufficient to give the accused grounds for supposing that by making it he would gain an advantage or avoid an evil of a temporal nature in reference to the proceedings against him .

What is a confession?

The "confession" has not been defined anywhere in the Act. A "confession" is an admission made at any time by a person charged with a crime, stating or suggesting the inference that he committed that crime.

Shahoo vs. State of UP, AIR 1966 SC

The Supreme Court held that before a confession can be accepted in evidence, it must be established by cogent evidence what were the exact words used by the accused. Even if so much is established, prudence and justice demand that such evidence cannot be made the sole ground of conviction. It may be used as a corroborative piece of evidence.

Definition:

Stephen: It is an admission made at any time by an accused stating and suggesting that he has committed the crime.

Stephen's definition condemned that stating crime has committed by accused is confession by suggesting of an inference is an admission only.

Therefore, the above definition suggested by Stephen was modified by the PC which held that only a direct acknowledgement of guilt should be regarded as a confession. A confession must either admit the offence or at least substantially all the fact which constitute crime. **[Pakala Narayan Swami vs. Emperor, AIR 1939]**

Confession must either be accepted as a whole or rejected as a whole and the Court is not competent to accept only the exculpatory part while rejecting the exculpatory part as incredible. **[Palvinder Singh Kaur vs. State of Punjab, AIR**

1952]

Hanumant v. State of M.P. 1952 SC

The apex court held than an admission made by a person whether amounting to a confession or not cannot be split up and part of it used against him. An admission must be used either as a whole or not at all.

When a confession is relevant

A confession is relevant -

a) If it is made after the impression caused by any such inducement, threat or promise has been fully removed);

b) If it is not made to a police officer;

c) If it is made in the presence of a Magistrate when the accused is in the custody of a police officer .

Before recording a confession: Giving warning that it will be used against the person making it is fundamental basic principle of criminal jurisprudence."

To be accepted as a whole or rejected as a whole

It is the well accepted rule regarding the used of confessions and admissions that there must be accepted as a whole or rejected as a whole and that the court is not competent to accept only the inculpatory part while rejecting the exculpatory part as inherently incredible. **[Palvinder Kaur vs. State of Punjab (1953) SCR]**

Nishi Kant Jha vs. State of Bihar, AIR 1969 SC

The Supreme Court held that where the exculpatory part of a confessional statement is not only inherently improbable but is contradicted by the other evidence, the court can accept only inculpatory part and piecing the same with the other evidence convict the accused. The court did not overrule Palvinder Kaur, Hanumant but distinguished the present case from them. In this case the explanation were inconsistent in themselves and also with the other evidences on record, and were therefore so obviously false that there was no chance of Justice being miscarried in discarding them.

Mohan Lal vs. Ajit Singh, AIR 1978 SC

The exculpatory part can be excluded where the evidence on record disproves it.

Keshoram Bora vs. Assam, AIR 1978 SC

The exculpatory part can be rejected and inculpatory part can be accepted when exculpatory part is apparently false.

Pyare Lal vs. State of Rajasthan, AIR 1963 SC

The Supreme Court has held that the mere existence of the threat, inducement or promise is not enough, but, in the opinion of the court, the said threat, inducement or promise shall be sufficient to cause a reasonable belief in the mind of the accused that by confessing he would get an advantage or avoid any evil of a temporal nature in reference to the proceedings against him, while the opinion is that of the court the criterion is the reasonable belief of the accused.

Khageswar Khatu vs. State, 1993 Cr.L.J. (SC)

It was held that Gram Rakhi (village caretaker) is not a police officer. Hence, confession before him is not inadmissible, if it is voluntary.

Retracted Confession:

A retracted confession, if proved to be voluntarily made, can be acted upon along with the other evidence in case and there is no legal requirement that a retracted confession must be supported by independent reliable evidence corroborating. It is material particular. The use to be made of such a confession is a matter of prudence rather than of law.

So, a confession is not to be regarded as involuntary merely because it is retracted later on.

Pyare Lal vs. State of Rajasthan, AIR 1963 - It was held by the open court that a retracted confession may form the legal basis of a conviction. If the court is satisfied that it was true and was voluntarily made.

Confession can be of two types:

1) Judicial Confession

2) Extra judicial confession

(1) Judicial Confession - which is recorded in front of a magistrate or court. It is more powerful that extra judicial confession.

(2) Extra Judicial Confession - Confessions are made either to the police or to any other person other than Judges and Magistrates as such. It is a very weak kind of evidence. It can be readied by the court along with other evidence.

Confession is a part of admission:

, there is not any separate heading for confession. It is covered under the heading of admission. So, it is a part of admission. Therefore, every confession is an admission but every admission is not confession and admission as defined is a statement. So, statement is genus. Admission is species and confession is sub-species.

COMMENTS

The comments mentioned under Section 22 of the Bharatiya Sakshya Adhiniyam, 2023 are based upon Section 24 of the Indian Evidence Act, 1872 (1 of 1872)

The Supreme Court in the case of Balvinder Singh v. State of Punjab, 1996 Cr...

883, held that where the alleged extra-judicial confession by the accused was surrounded by suspicious circumstances such as gross delay in lodging complaint with the police, the order of conviction for murder and tampering with evidence of the crime cannot be said to be sustainable on basis of alleged confession.

Balvinder Singh v. State of Punjab, 1996 Cr.L.]. 883.

The comments mentioned under Section 22 of the Bharatiya Sakshya Adhiniyam, 2023 are based upon Section 28 of the Indian Evidence Act, 1872 (1 of 1872)

Extra-judicial confession is a weak piece of evidence and the court must ensure that the same inspires confidence and is corroborated by other prosecution evidence. In order to accept extra-judicial confession, it must be voluntary and must inspire confidence. If the court is satisfied that the extra-judicial confession is voluntary, it can be acted upon to base the conviction.

Ram Lal v. State of Himachal Pradesh, AIR 2018 SC 4616.

The comments mentioned under Section 22 of the Bharatiya Sakshya Adhiniyam, 2023 are based upon Section 29 of the Indian Evidence Act, 1872 (1 of 1872)

Failure to comply with Section 164(3), CrPC or with High Court circulars will not render the confession inadmissible in evidence. Relevancy and admissibility of evidence have to be determined in accordance with the provisions of the Evidence Act.

Dagdu v. State of Maharashtra, AIR 1977 SC 1579.

23. Confession to police officer—(1) No confession made to a police officer shall be proved as against a person accused of any offence.

(2) No confession made by any person while he is in the custody of a police officer, unless it is made in the immediate presence of a Magistrate shall be proved against him:

Provided that when any fact is deposed to as discovered in consequence of information received from a person accused of any offence, in the custody of a police officer, so much of such information, whether it amounts to a confession or not, as relates distinctly to the fact discovered, may be proved.

COMMENTS

The comments mentioned under Section 23 (1) of Bharatiya Sakshya Adhiniyam, 2023 is based on Section 25 of Indian Evidence Act and Section 23(2) of the Bharatiya Sakshya Adhiniyam, 2023 are based upon Section 26 and 27 of the Indian Evidence Act, 1872 (1 of 1872).

Essential requirements

Mandatory requirements for the application of Section 27 of Evidence Act as follows: (i) the person giving information must be an accused of any offence and (ii) he must also be in police custody.

Boby v. State of Kerala, (2023) 1 SCR 335: 2023 INSC 23.

Admissibility of statement u/s 27 of the Evidence Act

Statement not liable to be rejected merely because it was recorded in a language not known to the accused through translator.

Siju Kurian v. State of Karnataka, AIR 2023 SC 2239.

That the confessional statement of the appellant stands and satisfies the test of section 27, where the appellant explained the way in which the accused committed the crime and shared the spoils. It is also came into light by his confession that the accused broke the doors of the house of informant with the aid of heavy stones and assaulted the inmates with pieces of wood. The recoveries of usedpolythene pouches of Wine, Money, Clothes, Chains and Bangle were all made at the disclosure by the accused which corroborates his confessional statement and proves his guilt.

Raju Manjhi v. State of Bihar, AIR 2018 SC 3592.

The comments mentioned under Section 23(2) of the Bharatiya Sakshya Adhiniyam, 2023 are based upon Section 26 of the Indian Evidence Act, 1872 (1 of 1872)

Confession whenever and wherever made to the police or while in the custody of the police to any person whomsoever, unless made in the immediate presence of a magistrate, shall be presumed to have been obtained under circumstances mentioned in Section 24 and admissible.

Commissioner of Police, New Delhi v. Narender Singh, AIR 2006 SC 1800.

INCULPATORY CONFESSION :- The confession where accuse directly admits his guilt is referred as an Inculpatory confession.

EXCULPATORY CONFESSION:- The confession which absolves the accused from his liability.

A. Nagesia vs. Bihar State, AIR 1966 SC

No part of a FIR lodged by the accused with the police could be admitted into evidence if it was in the nature of a confessional statement. The statement can be admitted to identify the aceused as the maker of the report.

Sita Ram vs. State of UP, AIR 1966 SC

A confession contained in a letter written and signed by the accused and addressed to a police-officer was held to be admissible as the letter was not written in the presence of the police officer.

Police Officer

This terms should not be read in a strict technical sense but according to its more comprehensive and popular meaning.

Raja Ram vs. State of Bihar, AIR 1964 SC

The Supreme Court has held that the test for determining whether a person is a police-officer for purposes of this section would be whether the powers of a police-officer which was conferred on him or which are exercisable by him establish a direct or substantial relationship with the prohibition enacted by this section, that is relating to the recording of a confession.

Custody

The mere temporary absence of policeman from the room in which confession is recorded does not terminate his custody of the accused , if he was taken effective steps to prevent his escape whether by locking the door of the room or by waiting outside .

Agnoo Nagesia vs state of Bihar

Supreme court held that the statement that the accused had committed the offence or that he had hidden the object at some place are not admissible what is admissible is only that portion of the statement which reveals the information about the place of hiding the object.

24. Consideration of proved confession affecting person making it and others jointly under trial for same offence.-When more persons than one are being tried jointly for the same offence, and a confession made by one of such persons affecting himself and some other of such persons is proved, the Court may take into consideration such confession as against such other person as well as against the person who makes such confession.

Explanation I.- "Offence", as used in this section, includes the abetment of, or attempt to commit, the offence.

Explanation II. -A trial of more persons than one held in the absence of the accused who has absconded or who fails to comply with a proclamation issued under section 84 of the Bharatiya Nagarik Suraksha Sanhita, 2023 shall be deemed to be a joint trial for the purpose of this section.

Illustrations

(a) A and B are jointly tried for the murder of C. It is proved that A said-"B and I murdered C". The Court may consider the effect of this confession as against B.

(b) A is on his trial for the murder of C. There is evidence to show that C was murdered by A and B, and that B said—"A and I murdered C". This statement may not be taken into consideration by the Court against A, as B is not being jointly tried.

Ingredients

Under this section, a confession by one person may be taken into consideration against another -

a) If both of them are tried jointly;

b) If they are tried for the same offence;

c) If the confession is legally proved;

Comment

Based on section 30 of Indian Evidence Act 1872 , this section says that where an accused person unreservedly confesses his own guilt, and at the same time, implicates another person who is jointly tried with him for the same offence, his confession may be taken into consideration against such other person as well as against himself, because the admission of his own guilt operates as a sort of sanction, which, to some extent, takes the place of the true one sanction of an oath and so affords some guarantee that the whole statement is a

- But this is a very weak guarantee. For a confession may be true so far as its maker is concerned, but may be false and concocted through malice so far as it affects others.

Weak Evidence

The Privy Council held **in Bhubani Sahu vs. The King, (1949) 76 1A 147** that a confession of a co-accused is obviously evidence of a very weak type. It does not come within the definition of "evidence" contained in Section 3. It is not required to be given on oath, nor in the presence of the accused, and it cannot be tested by cross-examination. It is a much weaker type of evidence than the evidence of an approver which is not subject to any of those infirmities.

Kashmira Singh vs. State of M.P., (1952) SCR 526

The Supreme Court has also held that the confession of an accused person against a co-accused is not evidence in the ordinary sense of the term. It does not come within the meaning of evidence contained in Section 3 of the

Evidence Act because

a) It is not required to be given on oath.

It is not required to be given in the presence of the co-accused against whom imputations are made.

c) It cannot be tested by cross-examination.

d) It may be false and concocted through malice as far as it affects others.

State of M.P. v. Paltan Mallah 2005 SC

Confession of co-accused implicating those who paid him to murder the trade union leader, not accepted because there was no other evidence against other.

Joint Trial

To apply this section, there should be a joint trial of the accused. The joint trial should be legal. If from any cause the accused who make the confession cannot be legally tried with the accused against whom the confession is to be used, the court should not attach any value to the confession.

Illustration (b) to Section 24 makes it clear - A is on his trial for the murder of

C. There is evidence to show that C was murdered by A and B, and that B said -

"A and I murdered C"

The statement may not be taken into consideration by the court against A, as B is not being jointly tried.

For the same offence

This expression means an offence coming under the same legal definition, i.e. under the same section of the law.

Confession made by one of such persons affecting himself and some other of such persons

Balbir Singh vs. State of Punjab, AIR 1957 SC

The Supreme Court has held that a confession must implicate the maker substantially to the same extent as the other accused person against whom it is sought to be taken into consideration.

25. Admissions not conclusive proof, but may estop.-Admissions are not conclusive proof of the matters admitted but they may operate as estoppels under the provisions hereinafter contained.

Ingredients

a) Admissions are not conclusive proof of the matters admitted.

b) But they may operate as estoppels.

Comment

Based on section 31 of Indian Evidence Act . this section declares that admissions are not conclusive proof of the matters admitted, but that they may operate as estoppels.

- Unless admissions are contractual or unless they constitute an estoppel they are not conclusive, but are open to rebuttal or explanation.

- A mere admission is conclusive only where it has been acted on by the party to whom it was made. An estoppel, i.e. a representation acted on by the other party, by creating a substantive right, does oblige the estopped party to make good his representation, in other words, it is conclusive.

Two other kinds of admissions may also be effective:

I) Admissions contained in the pleadings in a case which would circumscribe the issues and avoid the necessity for proof, and

ii) Admissions made by the parties to a suit on earlier occasions either in prior proceedings in a court of law, or in statements made out of court. What a party himself admits to be true may reasonably be presumed to be so.

Narayan vs. Gopal, AIR 1960 SC 100

The section says that an admission is not conclusive proof; it does not say that an admission is not sufficient proof without corroboration. It deals with the effect as to conclusiveness of an admission. The express admissions of a party to the suit or admissions implied from his conduct are strong evidence against him.

Difference between Estoppel and Admission

ESTOPPEL ADMISSION

Estoppel binds only parties It is not with admission . even

And privies thereto a stranger can take advantage

Of admission
Estoppel being a rule of An action can be founded on
Evidence , an action cannot an admission .
Be founded on it
It applies only in civil law generally , it also
Applies in civil law
Awadh Kishore Das vs. Ram Gopal, AIR 1979 SC 861

Admission made by a party in a previous suit binds the successors in interest and legal representatives in subsequent suit.

- The provisions of this section are not restricted to admissions made at any particular time or place, but are wide enough to include admissions made in pleadings .

26. Cases in which statement of relevant fact by person who is dead or cannot be found, etc., is relevant.- Statements, written or verbal, of relevant facts made by a person who is dead, or who cannot be found, or who has become incapable of giving evidence, or whose attendance cannot be procured without an amount of delay or expense which under the circumstances of the case appears to the Court unreasonable, are themselves relevant facts in the following cases, namely:—

(a) when the statement is made by a person as to the cause of his death, or as to any of the circumstances of the transaction which resulted in his death, in cases in which the cause of that person's death comes into question. Such statements are relevant whether the person who made them was or was not, at the time when they were made, under expectation of death, and whatever may be the nature of the proceeding in which the cause of his death comes into question;

(b) when the statement was made by such person in the ordinary course of business, and in particular when it consists of any entry or memorandum made by him in books kept in the ordinary course of business, or in the discharge of professional duty; or of an acknowledgement written or signed by him of the receipt of money, goods, securities or property of any kind; or of a document used in commerce written or signed by him; or of the date of a letter or other document usually dated, written or signed by him;

(c) when the statement is against the pecuniary or proprietary interest of the person making it, or when, if true, it would expose him or would have exposed him to a criminal prosecution or to a suit for damages;

(d) when the statement gives the opinion of any such person, as to the existence of any public right or custom or matter of public or general interest, of the existence of which, if it existed, he would have been likely to be aware, and when such statement was made before any controversy as to such right, custom or matter had arisen;

(e) when the statement relates to the existence of any relationship by blood, marriage or adoption between persons as to whose relationship by blood, marriage or adoption the person making the statement had special means of knowledge, and when the statement was made before the question in dispute was raised;

(f) when the statement relates to the existence of any relationship by blood, marriage or adoption between persons deceased, and is made in any will or deed relating to the affairs of the family to which any such deceased person belonged, or in any family pedigree, or upon any tombstone, family portrait or other thing on which such statements are usually made, and when such statement was made before the question in dispute was raised;

(g) when the statement is contained in any deed, will or other document which relates to any such transaction as is specified in clause (a) of section 11;

(h) when the statement was made by a number of persons, and expressed feelings or impressions on their part relevant to the matter in question.

Illustrations

(a) The question is , whether A was murdered by B ; or dies of injuries received in a transaction in the course of which she was raped. The question is whether she was raped by B; or the question is, whether A was killed by B under such circumstances that a suit would lie against B by A's widow.Statements made by A as to the cause of his or her death, referring respectively to the murder, the rape and the actionable wrong under consideration, are relevant facts.

(b) The question is as to the date of A's birth. An entry in the diary of a deceased surgeon regularly kept in the course of business, stating that, on a given day he attended A's mother and delivered her of a son, is a relevant fact.

(c) The question is, whether A was in Nagpur on a given day. A statement in the diary of a deceased solicitor, regularly kept in the course of business, that on a given day the solicitor attended A at a place mentioned, in Nagpur, for the purpose of conferring with him upon specified business, is a relevant facts.

(d) The question is, whether a ship sailed from Mumbai harbour on a given day. A letter written by a deceased member of a merchant's firm by which she was chartered to their correspondents in Chennai, to whom the cargo was consigned, stating that the ship sailed on a given day from Mumbai port, is a relevant fact.

(e) The question is, whether rent was paid to A for certain land. A letter from A's deceased agent to A, saying that he had received the rent on A's account and held it at A's orders is a relevant fact.

(f) The question is, whether A and B were legally married. The statement of a deceased clergyman that he married them under such circumstances that the celebration would be a crime is relevant.

(g) The question is, whether A, a person who cannot be found, wrote a letter on a certain day.

The fact that a letter written by him is dated on that day is relevant

(h) The question is , what was the cause of wreck of ship . A protest made by the captain , whose attendance cannot be procured , is a relevant fact

(i) The question is, whether a given road is a public way. A statement by A, a deceased headman of the village, that the road was public, is a relevant fact.

(j) The question is, what was the price of grain on a certain day in a particular market. A statement of the price, made by a deceased business person in the ordinary course of his business, is a relevant fact.

(k) The question is, whether A, who is dead, was the father of B. A statement by A that B was his son, is a relevant fact.

(l) The question, is, what was the date of the birth of A. A letter from A's deceased father to a friend, announcing the birth of A on a given day, is a relevant fact

(m) The question is, whether, and when, A and B were married. An entry in a memorandum book by C, the deceased father of B, of his daughter's marriage with A on a given date, is a relevant fact.

(n) A sues B for a libel expressed in a painted caricature exposed in a shop window. The question is as to the similarity of the caricature and its libellous character. The remarks of a crowd of spectators on these points may be proved.

COMMENT

The comment mentioned under Section 26 of the Bharatiya Sakshya Adhiniyam, 2023 are based upon Section 32 of the Indian Evidence Act, 1872 (1 of 1872)

A dying declaration made by a person as to cause of his/her death or as to any of the circumstances which resulted in his/her death, in cases in which cause of death comes in question is relevant under Section 32 of the Evidence Act. It has been emphasized number of times that dying declaration is an exception to the rule against admissibility of hearsay evidence. The whole development of the notion that the dying declaration as an exception to the hearsay rule is based on the formalistic view that the determination of certain classes of evidence as admissible or inadmissible and not on the apparent credibility of partioular evidence tendered.

Madan alias Madhu Patekar v. State of Maharashtra, AIR 2018 SC 2007.

Ingredients

A statement of relevant facts made by a person

a) who is dead;

b) who cannot be found;

c) who has become incapable of giving evidence;

d) whose attendance cannot be procured without unreasonable delay or expense,

is relevant under the following circumstances:

i) When it relates to the cause of his death.

ii) When it is made in the course of business; such as an entry in books, or acknowledgment of the receipt of any property, or date of a document.

iii. When it is against the pecuniary or proprietary interest of the person making it or when it would have exposed him to a criminal prosecution.

iv) When it gives opinion as to a public right or custom or matters of general interest and it was made before any controversy as to such right or custom had arisen.

v) When it relates to the existence of any relationship between persons as to whose relationship the maker had special means of knowledge and was made before the question in dispute arose.

vi) When it relates to the existence of any relationship between persons deceased and is made in any will or deed or family pedigree, or upon any tombstone or family-portrait, and was made before the question in dispute vii) When it is contained in any deed, will or other document. This clause, however, does not allow introduction of parole evidence.

Vili) When it is made by a number of persons and expresses feelings relevant to the matter in question.

Principle

Under this Section written or verbal statements of relevant facts made by a person -

a) Who is dead;

b) Who cannot be found;

c) Who has become incapable of giving evidences;

d) Whose attendance cannot be procured without unreasonable delay or expense;

Without unreasonable delay or expense are relevant under the following circumstances:

a) When it relates to the cause of his death (Clause 1)

b) Statements in course of business (Clause 2)

c) Statement against the interest of maker (Clause 3)

d) Opinion as to a public right or custom (Clause 4)

e) Statement as to existence of relationship between persons alive or dead (Clause 5)

f) Statement relating to relationship between deceased persons only (Clause 6)

g) Statements as to customary rights (Clause 7)

h) General remarks (Clause 8)

It is necessary that the above mentioned statements must be made before the question in dispute arose.

Cause of death (Clause 1)

When the statement is made by a person as (i) to the cause of his death or as ii) to any circumstances of the transaction which resulted in his dead, in cases in which the cause of that person's death comes into question.

Such statements are relevant whether the person who made them was or was not at the time when they were made, under expectation of death, and whatever may be the nature of the proceeding in which the cause of his death comes into question.

Dying-Declaration (Most Important)

The statements referred to in clause 1 are called 'dying declaration'. It has been discussed as below:

Meaning

Words "dying declaration" mean a statement written or verbal of relevant facts made by a person who is dead. It is dealt under clause (1) of Section 32 of the Indian Evidence Act, 1872. Generally, it relates to the cause of death of the declarant. "Dying declaration" can be proved by the person who records it. A dying declaration is not complete unless full names and addresses of the persons involved are given in it.

Definition of dying declaration by Addot CJ:

Dying declaration means the statement of a person who has died explaining the circumstances of his death.

R vs. Woodcock - A statement has been made when the person at the point of death where every hope of his world has gone (i.e. expectancy of death).

Difference between the English Law and Indian Law
English Law Indian Law
1-A dying declaration is relevant 1- such statement are
Only in criminal cases where admissible both in civil
The cause of death is in and criminal proceedings
Question . these are admissible even
If the trial is not for

2. **The dying declaration is person's death.**

Admissible only in a single 2- in India , cases of
Instance of homicide i.e. suicide are also covered .
Murder and manslaughter

3. **To be relevant , a dying 3- there is not any such**

Declaration must have been requirement in Bharatiya
Made in expectation in Sakshya Adhiniyam.
Death . a declaration
Made not appreciation
Of immediate or
Impending death would not
Be admitting.

4. **It is necessary that the 4- In India , if the deceased**

Deceased should have has narrated the full story
Completed his but fails to answer the last
Statement before dying formal question , the
Declaration can be relied
Upon.
Requirements:
According to Section 26 (1) itself:
1) Statement may be oral and written.
Emperor vs. Abdullah - Conduct was held to be relevant as dying declaration.
2) Statement must be as to:
(a) cause of death
(b) circumstances of the transaction
(c) resulted in the death

Pakala Narayan Swamy vs. Emperor, AIR 1939 - The statement made by the deceased to his wife that he was going to the accused to collect money from him (accused being indebted to the deceased), was held to be admissible under section 26

FIR as dying declaration - Where an injured person lodged the FIR and then died. It was held to be relevant as dying declaration. **[K. Ramchanda Reddy vs. Public Prosecution, (1976)]**

3) Death of the person is must while making the statement - If death is not the result, his statement inadmissible as dying declaration but it might be relied on to corroborate his testimony or to contradict him .

4) Cause of death of the deceased must be in question.

5) Expectancy of death is not necessary.

6) Whatever may be the nature of proceeding - It may be civil or criminal nature where the death of the person deceased is in question.

Sant Gopal vs. State of U.P., 1995 Cr.L.J. (All.)

Evidence of dying declaration is admissible not only against the person actually causing the death but also against other persons participating in causing death.

a. **Language of dying declaration**

Dying declaration recorded in the language of the declarant acquires added strength and reliability. As far as possible, it should be recorded in the exact words and language of the declarant.

Deepak Baliram Bajaj vs. State of Maharashtra, 1993 Cr.L.J. (SC)

In the above mentioned case of death of a lady due to 100% burn injuries, the dying declaration was recorded in hospital by a constable. Questions were asked in Sindhi by Special Executive Magistrate and were replied in Sindhi and then translated to the constable in Hindi who in turn recorded them in Marathi. The declaration was explained in Hindi and not in Sindhi to the declarant. The Supreme Court held that the conviction based solely on such a dying declaration could not be sustained.

Who can record a Dying declaration?

A dying declaration can be recorded by a person, even by a police-officer. But if it is recorded by a judicial Magistrate, it will have more strength and reliability.

State of U.P. vs. Shishupal Singh, AIR 1994 SC

The dying declaration was recorded by the Magistrate which was neither signed by the deceased, nor contained date and time of its recording and the prosecution failed to give any explanation that the deceased was not in a position to sign it, it was held that such dying declaration which was impregnate with so many suspicious circumstances which created doubt about its genuineness and it was not safe to base conviction on it.

Malik Ram Bhai vs. State of Orissa, 1993 Cr.L.J. (SC)

The dying declaration was recorded by the doctor in question and answer form in the presence of other witnesses and itwas corroborated with the testimony of other eye-witnesses. It was held that it was sufficient to convict the accused.

- Dying declaration recorded by police does not stand self-condemned but create suspicion. In emergency, it can be recorded without calling a Magistrate or doctor.

Ram Singh vs. Delhi Administration, 1995 Cr. L.J. (Delhi)

It was held by Delhi High Court that a clear and corroborated dying declaration cannot be rejected just only because it was recorded by a police officer.

Bhoora Singh vs. State of U.P., 1992 Cr.L.J. (All.)

In the case of a dowry death, it was held that dying declaration could not be rejected merely on the ground that it was made to the relatives of the deceased.

Form of dying declaration

It may be in the form of questions and answer or description generally, but not always, necessarily.

Rabi Chandra Pradhan vs. State of Orissa, AIR 1980 SC

The mere fact that a dying declaration is not in the form of question - answer does not destroy its value.

Fitness of declarant

Certificate from the doctor and endorsement from him that the victim was not only conscious but also in a fit condition to make a statement is a must. In the absence of such a certificate, the declaration may be rendered heavily suspect.

Amar Singh vs. State of M.P., 1996 Cr.L.J. (MP)

It was held by M.P. High Court that without proof of mental or physical fitness, the dying declaration was not reliable.

Hans Raj vs. State of Rajasthan, 1995 Cr.L.J. (Rajasthan)

The fact that the deceased had hundred per cent burn injuries of second degree and third degree, was not held to be sufficient to presume that the victim was not physically and mentally fit to give statements.

Proof of dying declaration

A dying declaration may be written or oral. It may be proved by the evidence of a witness who had it made. When a dying declaration is recorded by a magistrate , it must be proved by calling the magistrate as witness .

State of Assam vs. M. Ahmed, AIR 1983 SC

A dying declaration is not a proof of the truth of its contents but only of the fact stated. If it is truthful, it can be the sole basis of conviction when it is not properly proved it cannot be used to corroborate other evidence.

Admissibility of statements

There are certain pre-requisites to the admissibility of a statement under this section. The court has to be convinced that the witness whose statement is offered is dead, or cannot be found, or has become incapable of giving evidence or unreasonable delay or expense is involved in producing him.

Non-examination of scribe

It is necessary that the scribe must be produced in the court. The accused should also be given a chance to cross-examine him.

Govind Narain vs. State of Rajasthan, AIR 1993 SC

The alleged dying declaration was reduced into writing but the scribe was neither examined nor cross-examined and the prosecution failed to explain the cause for non-production of the scribe. It was held that the declaration was liable to be discarded

More than one dying declaration

When there are more than one dying declarations of the same person, they have to be read as one and the same statement for proper appreciation of the value and, if they differ from each other on material aspects the effort should be made to see if they could be reconciled. If no assumption could explain the difference, the statements might become unworthy of credit but if one is possible the position may be different.

Harbans Lal vs. State of Haryana, 1993 Cr.L.J. (SC)

In the above mentioned case of bride burning, two dying declarations were produced. One was duly recorded by a doctor in the presence of two other doctors stating that she was burnt by her mother-in-law and husband. The other was recorded by some person attested by the Sarpanch stating that she had committed suicide. The latter was not proved by competent witness. It was held that the latter could not be relied upon.

If the declarant chances to live

If the dying declarant does not die, his declaration cannot be used under Section 26 (1) as dying declaration.

Appabhai vs. State of Gujarat, AIR, 1988 SC

If a person making a dying declaration chances to live, his statement is inadmissible as a dying declaration under Section 26(1), but it might be relied upon under the provisions to corroborate his testimony when examined.

The following are the consequences if the declarant does not dies:

i. A dying declaration under Section 26 (1) is admissible only when the death of the declarant is proved.
ii. If the declarant survives , his declaration is inadmissible under section 26(1)
iii. He should be examined in the court and the adverse party must be given a chance to cross examine him
iv. His testimony should be used for corroboration
v. It can be contradicted by the adverse party.

Admissibility of dying declaration

The Supreme Court has laid down in several judgments the principles governing dying declaration, which can be summed up as under.

i. There is neither rule of law nor of prudence that the dying declaration cannot be acted upon without corroboration.

ii. If the court is satisfied that the dying declaration is true and voluntary, it can base conviction on it, without corroboration.
iii. The court has to scrutinise the dying declaration carefully and must ensure that the declaration is not the result of tutoring, prompting or imagination. The deceased had opportunity to observe and identify the assailants and was in a fit state to make the declaration.

iv) Where dying declaration is suspicious it should not be acted upon without corroborative evidence.

V) Where the deceased was unconscious and could never make any dying declaration the evidence with regard to it is to be rejected.

Vi) A dying declaration which suffers from infirmity cannot form the basis of conviction.

vii) Merely because a dying declaration does not contain the details as to the occurrence, it is not to be rejected.

viii) Equally, merely because it is a brief statement it is not to be discarded, on the contrary, the shortness of the statement itself guarantees truth.

ix) Normally, the court in order to satisfy whether deceased was in a fit mental condition to make the dying declaration look up to medical opinion. But where the eyewitness has said that the deceased was in a fit and conscious state to make the dying declaration, the medical opinion cannot prevail.

x) Where the prosecution version differs from the version as given in the dying declaration, the said declaration cannot be acted upon.

Kamla vs. State of Punjab, AIR 1993, SC

A dying declaration stated two stab injuries, medical report showed only one injury. Inconsistency destroyed the value of the dying declaration (held).

Some other important case law

Pakala Narayana Swami vs. King Emperor

The appellant was charged with the offence of murder. The body of the deceased which was cut was recovered from a trunk in a railway compartment

on March 23, 1937. One of the items of evidence against him adduced by the prosecution was a statement by the deceased to his wife on March 20, 1937 that he received a letter asking him to go to the house of the accused for receiving money due to him and that he was so going. On the question of its admissibility in evidence, the Privy Council observed:

"The statement was rightly admitted under Section 26(1) of the Evidence Act.

For admissibility under the section, the statement may be made before the cause of death has arisen, or before the deceased has any reason to anticipate being killed. The circumstances must be circumstances of the transaction: general expressions indicating fear or suspicion whether of a particular individual or otherwise and not directly related to the occasion of the death will not be admissible. But statements made by the deceased that he was proceeding to the spot where he was in fact killed, or as to his reason for so proceeding, or that he was going to meet a particular person, or that he had been invited by such person to meet him would each of them be circumstances of the transaction, and would be so whether the person was unknown, or was not the person accused. Such a statement might indeed be exculpatory of the person accused. 'Circumstances of the transaction' is a phrase that no doubt conveys some limitation. It is not as broad as the analogous use in 'circumstantial evidence' which includes evidence of all relevant facts.

It is one the other hand narrower than 'res gestae'.

Circumstances must have some proximate relation to the actual occurrence; though, as for instance, in a case of prolonged poisoning they may be related to dates at a considerable distance from the date of the actual fatal dose. It will be observed that 'circumstances' are of the transaction which resulted in the death of the declarant. It is not necessary that there should be a known transaction other than that the death of the declarant has ultimately been caused, for the condition of the admissibility of the evidence is that the cause of (the declarant's) death comes into question. In the present case the cause of the deceased's death comes into question. The transaction is in which the deceased was murdered on March 21 or 22: and his body was found in a trunk proved to be bought on behalf of the accused. The statement made by the deceased on March 20 or 21 that he was setting out to the place where the accused lived, and to meet a person, the wife of the accused, who lived in the accused's house, appears clearly to be a statement as to some of the circumstances of the transaction which resulted in his death."

Bakshish Singh vs. State of Punjab

The appellant was convicted of murder on the basis of a dying declaration made by the victim. Though the deceased spoke in Punjabi, it was recorded in Urdu and was a long document and was narrative of a large number of incidents which happened before the actual assault. On the question of its admissibility, the Supreme Court said:

"(1) In Punjab the language used in the subordinate courts and that employed by the police for recording of statements has always been Urdu and the recording of the dying declaration in Urdu cannot be a ground for saying that the statement does not correctly reproduce what was stated by the declarant. This was a wholly inadequate reason for rejecting the dying declaration.

(2) Such a long statement is more in the nature of a first information report than a recital of the cause of death or circumstances resulting in it and is likely to give the impression that it was not genuine or not having been made unaided and without prompting. The dying declaration is the statement made by a person as to the cause of his death or as to any of the circumstances of the transaction which resulted in his death and such details which fall outside the ambit of this are not strictly within the permissible limits laid down in Section 26(1) of the Evidence Act, and unless absolutely necessary to make a statement coherent or complete, should not be included in the statement. In Punjab, no rules have been made in regard to the recording of dying declaration which has been done in several other States. It would be desirable if some such rules were framed and included in the rules and Orders made by the High Court for guidance of person recording dying declarations. Of course the authenticity of the dying declaration has to be judged in accordance with the circumstances of each case depending upon many factors which would vary with each case but those recording such statements would be well advised to keep in view the fact that the object of a dying declaration is to get from the person making the statement of the cause of death or the circumstances of the transaction which resulted in death."

Taking into consideration all the circumstances of the case, the Court acted on the dying declaration and confirmed the conviction.

Ratan Gond vs. State of Bihar

The accused was charged with the offence of murder. The items of evidence against him were: 0) statement of the victims sister (who died subsequently, but before the committal proceedings) as a result of which the victim's dead body was recovered; and (il) the confession of the accused before the panchayat officers. The Supreme Court held, with respect to item

"The statements of Aghami who unfortunately died within a few months of the occurrence before her statement could be recorded in a judicial proceeding were not admissible under Section 26 or Section 27 of the Act. Section 27 is clearly out of the way because the sister made no statements in a judicial proceeding or before any person authorised by law to take her evidence. The only relevant clause of Section 26 which may be said to have any bearing is clause (1) which relates to statements made by a person as to the cause of his death or as to any of the circumstances of the transaction which resulted in his death. In the case before us, the statements made by the sister do not relate to the cause of her death or to any of the circumstances relating to her death; on the contrary the statements relate to the death of her sister. Therefore, the statements do not come within Section 26(1) of the Evidence Act."

Moti Singh vs. State of UP

The accused was convicted on the dying declaration of a person who received two gunshot wounds during the occurrence. The dying declaration was given while the person was in hospital, but he died 20 days after he left the hospital, and there was no evidence that he died as a result of the injuries received at the incident. On the question of the admissibility of the dying declaration, the Supreme Court held:

"Clause (1) of Section 26 makes a statement of a person who has died relevant only when that statement is made by a person as to the cause of his death or as to any of the circumstances of the transaction which resulted in his death in cases in which the cause of that person's death comes into question. When the dead person in the present case is not proved to have died as a result of the injuries received in the incident his statement cannot be said to be statement as to the cause of his death or as to any of the circumstances of the transaction which resulted in his death..... The result is that the statement of the victim is inadmissible in evidence."

Khushal Rao vs. State of Bombay

The appellant was convicted for the offence of murder only on the basis of the dying declaration of the victim. The Supreme Court while dismissing the appeal laid down the following rules:

"(1) The provisions of Section 26(1) have been made by the Legislature, advisedly, as a matter of sheer necessity by way of an exception to the general rule that hearsay is no evidence and that evidence which has not been tested by cross-examination, is not admissible. The purpose of cross-examination is to test the veracity of the statements made by a witness. In the view of the Legislature, that test is supplied by the solemn occasion when it was made, namely, at a time when the person making the statement was in danger of losing his life. At such a serious and solemn moment, that person is not expected to tell lies; and secondly, the test of cross-examination would not be available. In such a case the necessity of oath also has been dispensed with for the same reasons.

Thus, a statement made by a dying person as to the cause of his death has been accorded by the Legislature a special sanctity which should, on first principles, be respected unless there are clear circumstances brought out in the evidence to show that the person making the statement was not in the expectation of death, not that that circumstance would affect the admissibility of the statement, but only its weight. It may also be shown by evidence that a dying declaration is not reliable because it was not made at the earlier opportunity, and thus, there was a reasonable ground to believe its having been put into the mouth of the dying man, when his resistance against telling a falsehood was ebbing away; or because the statement has not been properly recorded, for example, the statement has been recorded as a result of prompting by some interested parties, or was in answer to leading questions put by the recording officer, or by the person purporting to reproduce that statement. These may be some of the circumstances which can be said to detract from the value of a dying declaration.

(2) It cannot be laid down as an absolute rule of law that a dying declaration cannot form the sole basis of conviction unless it is corroborated.

(3) Each case must be determined on its own facts keeping in view the circumstances in which the dying declaration was made.

(4) It cannot be laid down as a general proposition that a dying declaration is a weaker kind of evidence.

(5) A dying declaration stands on the same footing as another piece of evidence and has to be judged in the light of surrounding circumstances and with reference to the principles governing the weighing of evidence.

(6) A dying declaration which has been recorded by a competent Magistrate in the proper manner, that is to say, in the form of questions and answers, and, as far as practicable in the words of the maker of the dying declaration, stands on a much higher footing than a dying declaration which depends upon oral testimony which may suffer from all the infirmities of human memory and human character.

(7) In order to test the reliability of a dying declaration, the court has to keep in view the circumstances like the opportunity of the dying man for observation, for example, whether there was sufficient light if the crime was committed at night; whether the capacity of the man to remember the facts stated had not been impaired at the time he was making the statement by circumstances beyond his control; that the statement has been consistent throughout if he had several opportunities of making a dying declaration apart from the official record of it; and that the statement has been made at the earliest opportunity and was not the result of tutoring by interested parties.

(8) A dying declaration cannot be made to equate with the evidence of an accomplice or the evidence furnished by a confession as against the maker, if it is retracted, and as against the others even though not retracted.

(9) The observation in **Madho Prasad vs. State of M.P.**, that: 'It is settled law that it is not safe to convict an accused person merely on the evidence furnished by a dying declaration without further corroboration because such a statement is not made an oath and is not subject to cross-examination and because the maker of it might be mentally and physically in a state of confusion and might well be drawing on his imagination while he was making the declaration', are in the nature of obiter dicta."

Queen Empress vs. Abdullah

The accused was charged with the murder of a prostitute by cutting her throat with a razor. When she was taken to the police station and shortly before her death, she was questioned by various persons as to the circumstances in which the injury had been inflicted on her, but she was unable to speak. She was, however, conscious and able to make signs.

Evidence was offered by the prosecution to prove the questions put to her and the signs she made in answer. Objection was taken on behalf of the accused that under Section 26 only written or verbal (or oral) statements made by a deceased as to the cause of his or her death were admissible and that the signs were not verbal within the meaning of the section.

It was held that the questions and the signs taken together might be regarded as verbal statements made by a person as to the cause of death within the meaning of Section 26 of the Act and, therefore, admissible. The signs could not be proved as conduct under Section 6 and its second Explanation, as taken alone, and without reference to the questions leading to them; there was nothing to connect with the cause of death. The conduct made relevant by Section 6 is conduct which is directly and immediately influenced by a fact in issue or relevant fact and it does not include actions resulting from some intermediate cause such as questions or suggestions by other persons. But Mr. Justice Mahmood held:

"The word "conduct in Section 6 does not mean only such conduct as is directly and immediately influenced by a fact in issue or relevant fact. The signs were the conduct of a person 'an offence against whom was the subject of any proceeding' and were relevant under Section 6. There remains the question whether the questions put to her were admissible, and whether she can be considered to have adopted the statements which they replied. Now Explanation 2 to Section 6 provides that: 'When the conduct of any person is relevant, any statement made to him or in his presence and hearing, which affect such conduct, is relevant.' I confess that I am quite unable to hold that for 'when' you must read 'before'. If you read the section as I do, the law stands thus: The conduct of the person, an offence against whom is being investigated, is relevant. The question whether it is intelligible or not arise afterwards, and the only way of ascertaining its meaning is to admit what Explanation 2 says may be admitted, namely, statements made to, or in the presence and hearing of, the person and which affect his conduct. This can only be done by taking the questions word for word, so as to explain the meaning of the conduct which they affected.

Finally, if Section 6, with the Explanations contained in it, were not sufficient to justify the view which I take of the question referred to the Full Bench, I should have relied on the provisions of Section 7, in order to allow an explanation of the meaning of the signs."

R vs. Bedingfield

On a trial for murder, it appeared that the deceased with her throat cut, came suddenly out of a room, in which she had left the prisoner, and that she said, immediately after coming out of the room and shortly before she died,

"See what Harry had done to me". It was held that her statement was not admissible in evidence, either as a dying declaration, as it did not appear that she was in fear of death; or as res gestae, as it was made after the transaction was complete.

A statement, in order to be admissible in evidence as part of the transaction or res gestae, must strictly accompany, or be made at the same time, as the physical acts in question.

The statement could not be viewed as conduct as, even if it is a complaint, the only complaints relevant under English law being complaints in sexual offences.

The statement would have been admissible under the Indian Evidence Act, Section 26 , as the condition that it should have been made with the feeling that death was imminent is not a condition under the Act.

Statements in course of business (Clause 2)

When it is made in the course of business, such as, entry in books, or acknowledgement or the receipt of any property, or date of a document, it is relevant. This clause contemplates a statement by a person whose duty it was to make such a statement or whose business was such that statements of the kind were to be expected in the ordinary course of things.

Clause (2) provides that a written statement of a relevant fact made by a person who is dead is itself a relevant fact, when the statement was made by such person in the ordinary course of business. The expression "course of business" occurs in more than one place in the Act.

The phrase "in the ordinary course of business" is apparently used to indicate the current routine of business which was usually followed by the person whose declaration it is sought to introduce.

Statement against the interest of maker (Clause 3)

A statement of a deceased person in order to be admissible under this clause must be a statement of a relevant fact and must be against the proprietary or pecuniary interest of the person making it.

Bhim Singh vs. Kan Singh, AIR 1980 SC

Before a statement can be admissible under this clause it must be shown that the person making it knew that it was against his pecuniary or proprietary interest.

In most cases such knowledge would have to be inferred from the surrounding circumstances. A statement by a person having proprietary interest in the suit property about benami holding which was against his own interest was held to be provable.

This clause comprises three classes of declarations against interest: where they affect the declarant's (1) pecuniary interest; (2) proprietary interest; and (3) personal liberty or property by tending to charge him with a crime or to subject him to payment of damages.

Opinion as to Public Right or Custom (Clause 4)

The admissibility of declarations of deceased persons in cases of public right or custom, or matters of public or general interest is allowed, as these rights or customs are generally of ancient and obscure origin and may be acted upon only at distant intervals of time; direct proof of their existence is not, therefore, demanded.

Keshow Prasad vs. Bhagjogna Kaer (1937) Bom LR (PC) A map prepared by a person, who is dead, in a previous case not inter partes, showing the limits of a particular district, is not admissible as it is not a matter of public or general interest within the meaning of this clause.

State of Bihar vs. Radha Krishan Singh, AIR 1983 SC

The declaration should have been made **ante litammotam** i.e. before the beginning of any controversy and not simply before the commencement of any suit involving the same subject-matter. The operation of bias is thus excluded.

Statement as to existence of relationship (Clause 5)

Statements relating to the existence of any relationship between persons alive or dead as to whose relationship the declarant has special means of knowledge are admissible if they are made before the question in dispute was raised.

K.V. Subbaraju vs. C. Subbaraju, AIR 1968 SC

"Before the question in dispute was raised" words do not necessarily mean before the dispute was raised in the particular litigation in which such a statement is sought to be adduced in evidence, that is the declarations are required to have been made not merely before the commencement of legal proceeding but before even the existence of any actual controversy concerning the subject-matter of the declarations.

Surjan vs. Sardar, (1900) 2 Bom LR 942: 27 1A 183: 23 All 72

The plaintiff, to prove his relationship, produced a pedigree which was prepared from the statements of bards and papers produced by them, some time ago by a Raja to settle the class of Thakurs to which he belonged. It was held that the pedigree was not admissible; since neither any of the bards nor the Raja who assembled the bards of the family and with their assistance had the pedigree drawn up was called as a witness and no proof was given that they were within any of the descriptions given by this section which made it unnecessary to call them.

Difference between clauses (5) and (6) [Clause 6]

Clause (5) refers to statements relating to the existence of any relationship between persons alive or dead and the statement is to be made by a person who had special means of knowledge, that is, it imposes the restriction that the person making the statement should have special means of knowledge.

Clause (6) refers to the existence of relationship between deceased persons only; and it imposes no such restriction as under clause (5). It is enough if the statement is made in a will or deed relating to the affairs of the family or in any family pedigree, etc., no matter by whom it was made.

Clause (6) also refers to pedigree, but differs from clause (5) in this - that in clause (5) the evidence is the declaration of the person deceased or otherwise unproduceable, in clause (6) the evidence is that of things, such as geneological trees, lambstones, etc. The statements in clause (5) may be either written or verbal; the statement in clause (6) must always be written as evidence therein is that of things.

Statements as to customary rights (Clause 7)

A statement contained in any deed, will, or other document which relates to a transaction by which a right, or custom in question was created, modified, recognised, asserted, or denied, is admissible under this clause. A statement in any relevant document, however recent, and though not more than thirty years old, is admissible.

Dwarka Nath vs. Lalchand, AIR 1955 SC

The word verbal used in beginning of this section naturally does not apply to this clause as well. This clause does not allow introduction of parole evidence.

General Remarks (Clause 8)

When a number of persons assemble together to give vent to one common statement, which statement expresses the feelings or impressions made in their minds at the time of making it, that statement may be repeated by the witnesses, and is evidence.

27. Relevancy of certain evidence for proving, in subsequent proceeding, truth of facts therein stated.-Evidence given by a witness in a judicial proceeding, or before any person authorised by law to take it, is relevant for the purpose of proving, in a subsequent judicial proceeding, or in a later stage of the same judicial proceeding, the truth of the facts which it states, when the witness is dead or cannot be found, or is incapable of giving evidence, or is kept out of the way by the adverse party, or if his presence cannot be obtained without an amount of delay or expense which, under the circumstances of the case, the Court considers unreasonable:

Provided that the proceeding was between the same parties or their representatives in interest; that the adverse party in the first proceeding had the right and opportunity to cross-examine and the questions in issue were substantially the same in the first as in the second proceeding.

Explanation.—A criminal trial or inquiry shall be deemed to be a proceeding between the prosecutor and the accused within the meaning of this section.

Ingredients

Evidence given by a witness (i) in a judicial proceeding, or (ii) before any person authorised by law to take it, is relevant in a subsequent judicial proceeding or a later stage of the same proceeding -

a) When the witness is dead,

b) When he cannot be found,

c) When he is incapable of giving evidence

d) When he is kept out of the way by the adverse party, or

e) When his presence cannot be obtained without an amount of delay or expense which the court considers unreasonable.

But such evidence will be admissible only –

a) If the proceeding was between the same parties, or their representatives in interest,

b) If the adverse party in the first proceeding had the right and opportunity to cross-examine; and

c) If the question in issue were substantially the same in the first as in the second proceeding.

Ghulam Haidar vs. The Crown (1929) Lah

It is only in cases where the production of primary evidence is beyond the party's power that secondary evidence of oral testimony is admissible. Noncompliance with the provisions of this section is not cured by the fact that counsel for the accused gives his consent thereto.

It provides that if it is proved that an accused person has absconded, and that there is no immediate prospect of arresting him, the court may try or commit for trial such person for the offence complained of and may, in his absence, examine the witnesses produced on behalf of the prosecution, and record their depositions and that such depositions may be used at the subsequent trial of the absconder, if the witnesses are dead or otherwise incapable of appearing.

Criminal trial or inquiry, deemed proceeding (Explanation)

The explanation is intended to do away with the objection that, in criminal cases, the state is the prosecutor. The effect of the explanation is that the deposition taken in criminal proceedings may be used in civil suit, and vice versa.

[Emperor vs. Mohammed Yusuf, (1932) Bom LR]

> Other Case laws (Section 27)

Reddi, (1881) 3 Mad 48

R charged A with breach of trust, and S gave evidence in support of the charge. A being acquitted, R was tried for making a false charge and S for perjury. It was held that the depositions given by witnesses in the first case could be used against R in the second case, but not against s under this section.

Foolkissory Dasee vs. Nobin Chunder Bhujno, (1895) 23 Cal 441

A prosecution was instituted by S against N at the instance and on behalf of F for criminal trespass in respect of a certain house, and on his own behalf for assault and insult. S gave evidence at the trial in support of those charges. F subsequently brought a civil suit against N for possession of the same house under Section 9 of the Specific Relief Act. S died before the institution of the civil suit. At the trial of the civil suit the deposition of S in the criminal Court was tendered by F as evidence on the issue of possession. It was held that, S being dead and the proceedings being between the same parties and the issues being substantially the same, the deposition of S was admissible.

COMMENT

The comment mentioned under Section 27 of the Bharatiya Sakshya Adhiniyam, 2023 are based upon Section 33 of the Indian Evidence Act, 1872 (1 of 1872)

The statement of witness recorded during the course of enquiry under Section 202 of the code cannot be used against the accused for any purpose as the same is not admissible under either under Section 33 or Section 157 of the Evidence Act and the same cannot be the basis of conviction of the accused.

Sashi Jena v. Khadal Swain, 2004 (48) ACC 644 (SC).

28. Entries in books of account when relevant.-Entries in the books of account, including those maintained in an electronic form, regularly kept in the course of business are relevant whenever they refer to a matter into which the Court has to inquire, but such statements shall not alone be sufficient evidence to charge any person with liability.

Illustration

A sues B for one thousand rupees, and shows entries in his account books showing B to be indebted to him to this amount. The entries are relevant, but are not sufficient, without other evidence, to prove the debt.

Entries in the diary **("Jain Hawala Diary Case")** showing certain payments made to a political leader were not admitted as evidence. The diary showed no dates on which the payments were supposed to have been made. Such diary cannot be regarded as a book maintained in the regular course of **business [L.K. Advani vs. CBI, 1997 Cr.L.J. 2556 (Delhi)].** Entries, even if relevant, are only corroborative evidence. Independent evidence, like the evidence of a transaction which brought about the entry, as to the trustworthiness of the entry would be necessary to fasten anybody with liability **[CBI vs. V.C. Shuk/a (1998) 3 SCC 410].**

Comment :- Based on section 34 of Indian Evidence Act

29. Relevancy of entry in public record or an electronic record made in performance of duty.-An entry in any public or other official book, register or record or an electronic record, stating a fact in issue or relevant fact, and made by a public servant in the discharge of his official duty, or by any other person in performance of a duty specially enjoined by the law of the country in which such book, register or record or an electronic record, is kept, is itself a relevant fact.

Section 29 is based upon the principle that public records maintained in the performance of official duties must carry a prima facie evidentiary value of their correctness. Thus, a municipal record of a person's date of birth or death is relevant to prove the date of birth or death of person concerned. There is, however, no presumption that such entries reflect only the truth. Though school register is relevant for showing date of birth, but in the absence of the material on the basis of which the entry was made, it would not be of much evidentiary value **(Birad Mal Singhvi vs.**

Anand Purohit AIR 1988 SC 1976). A statement of age in the pleadings of a party has been regarded as an evidence of his age.

COMMENT

The comment mentioned under Section 29 of the Bharatiya Sakshya Adhiniyam, 2023 are based upon Section 35 of the Indian Evidence Act, 1872 (1 of 1872)

It is not necessary that public document should be kept only by public officer, the only requirement is that it should be regularly kept in discharge of official duty. Hence certificate of higher secondary examination held to be a public document.

Umesh Chandra v. State of Rajasthan, AIR 1982 SC 1057.

30. Relevancy of statements in maps, charts and plans.-Statements of facts in issue or relevant facts, made in published maps or charts generally offered for public sale, or in maps or plans made under the authority of the Central Government or any State Government, as to matters usually represented or stated in such maps, charts or plans, are themselves relevant facts.

31. Relevancy of statement as to fact of public nature contained in certain Acts or notifications.-When the Court has to form an opinion as to the existence of any fact of a public nature, any statement of it, made in a recital contained in any Central Act or State Act or in a Central Government or State Government notification appearing in the respective Official Gazette or in any printed paper or in electronic or digital form purporting to be such Gazette, is a relevant fact.

32. Relevancy of statements as to any law contained in law books including electronic or digital form.-When the Court has to form an opinion as to a law of any country, any statement of such law contained in a book purporting to be printed or published including in electronic or digital form under the authority of the Government of such country and to contain any such law, and any report of a ruling of the Courts of such country contained in a book including inelectronic or digital form purporting to be a report of such rulings, is relevant.

33. What evidence to be given when statement forms part of a conversation, document, electronic record, book or series of letters or papers.-When any statement of which evidence is given forms part of a longer statement, or of a conversation or part of an isolated document, or is contained in a document which forms part of a book, or is contained in part of electronic record or of a connected series of letters or papers, evidence shall be given of so much and no more of the statement, conversation, document, electronic record, book or series of letters or papers as the Court considers necessary in that particular case to the full understanding of the nature and effect of the statement, and of the circumstances under which it was made.

34. Previous judgments relevant to bar a second suit or trial.-The existence of any judgment, order or decree which by law prevents any Court from taking cognizance of a suit or holding a trial, is a relevant fact when the question is whether such Court ought to take cognizance of such suit or to hold such trial.

Ingredients

i) the existence of any (a) judgment, (b) order or (c) decree

ii) which by law prevents any Court from (a) taking cognizance of a suit or (b) holding a trial

iii) is a relevant fact

iv. when the question is (a) whether such court ought to take cognizance of such suit or (b) to hold such trial.

Res-Judicata

The doctrine of res-judicata in its wider sense, Which includes a bar on the subsequent litigation not only of all issues resolved in the earlier proceedings but also of every point which properly belongs to the subject - matter of the litigation applies only when the course of action or issue is or remains between the saves parties or their predecessors in title and does not extend to those not themselves party to the earlier proceedings

The principle of this Section applies to Criminal Courts as well. The plea of aurefais convict or autrefais acquit, that is, of a previous lawful conviction or lawful acquittal, has always been held to be a good plea.

P.G. Eshwarappa v. M. Rydrappa 1996 SC

Principle of estoppel or res judicata do not apply when that would contravene some statutory direction or prohibition. This is something which cannot be overridden or defeated by a previous Judgement between the parties.

Guru Granth Saheb Sthan v. Meerghat Vanaras 2013 SC

Where there were both Civil and Criminal Proceeding instituted on the same cause and an application was made for stay of the civil suit, it was held that there was only the mere chance of conflicting decisions and that was not a sufficient ground for stay of the civil suit.

35. Relevancy of certain judgments in probate, etc., jurisdiction.—(1) A final judgment, order or decree of a competent Court or Tribunal, in the exercise of probate, matrimonial, admiralty or insolvency jurisdiction, which confers upon or takes away from any person any legal character, or which declares any person to be entitled to any such character, or to be entitled to any specific thing, not as against any specified person but absolutely, is relevant when the existence of any such legal character, or the title of any such person to any such thing, is relevant.

(2) Such judgment, order or decree is conclusive proof that—

(i) any legal character, which it confers accrued at the time when such judgment, order or decree came into operation;

(ii) any legal character, to which it declares any such person to be entitled, accrued to that person at the time when such judgment, order or decree declares it to have accrued to that person;

(iii) any legal character which it takes away from any such person ceased at the time from which such judgment, order or decree declared that it had ceased or should cease; and

iii. anything to which it declares any person to be so entitled was the property of that person at the time from which such judgment, order or decree declares that it had been or should be his property.

Ingredients

A final judgment of a Court exercising (1) probate, (2) matrimonial, (3) admiralty (4) insolvency jurisdiction which - (i) confers upon or takes away from any person any legal character, or (ii) declares any person to be entitled to (a) any such character, or (b) any specific thing absolutely, is relevant when (a) the existence of any such legal character, or (b) the title of any such person to any thing is relevant.

Such judgments are known as judgments in rem.

Such judgment is conclusive proof:

(i)That any legal character, which it confers, accrued at the time when such judgment came into operation.

ii) That any legal character to which it declares any person to be entitled accrued at the time mentioned in the judgment.

iii) That any legal character which it takes away from any person ceased at the time mentioned in the judgment.

Iv) That any thing to which it declares a person to be entitled was the person's property at the time at which the judgment declares it is to be his.

When a Judgment in rem can be impeached

A judgment in rem can only be impeached on the following grounds:

i. that the Court has no jurisdiction; or
ii. that the judgment was obtained by fraud or collusion; or
iii. that it was not given on the merits; or
iv. that it was not final, e.g. interlocutory.

* Judgment in rem is conclusive against all the world as to that status, whereas judgment in personam is only conclusive between the parties and privies.

Vishwanathan v. Abdul Wajid, AIR 1963 SC

Once a judgment falls within the Section, law dispenses with the proof of the legal character which it confers or declares together with the declarations of property arising from that legal character.

Satya v. Teja Singh, AIR 1975 SC

The Supreme Court held that the judgment of a foreign competent Court can be challenged on the ground of fraud.

36. Relevancy and effect of judgments, orders or decrees, other than those mentioned in section 35.-Judgments, orders or decrees other than those mentioned in section 35 are relevant if they relate to matters of a public naturerelevant to the enquiry; but such judgments, orders or decrees are not conclusive proof of that which they state.

Illustration

A sues B for trespass on his land. B alleges the existence of a public right of way over the land, which A denies. The existence of a decree in favour of the defendant, in a suit by A against C for a trespass on the same land, in which C alleged the existence of the same right of way, is relevant, but it is not conclusive proof that the right of way exists.

Ingredients

i) judgement relating to matters of a public nature are relevant

ii) through such judgement are not conclusive proof of what they state .

37. Judgments, etc., other than those mentioned in sections 34, 35 and 36 when relevant.-Judgments or orders or decrees, other than those mentioned in sections 34, 35 and 36, are irrelevant, unless the existence of such judgment, order or decree is a fact in issue, or is relevant under some other provision of this Adhiniyam.

Illustrations

(a) A and B separately sue C for a libel which reflects upon each of them. C in each case says that the matter alleged to be libellous is true, and the circumstances are such that it is probably true in each case, or in neither. A obtains a decreeagainst C for damages on the ground that C failed to make out his justification. The fact is irrelevant as between B and C.

(b) A prosecutes B for stealing a cow from him. B is convicted. A afterwards sues C for the cow, which B had sold to him before his conviction. As between A and C, the judgment against B is irrelevant.

(c) A has obtained a decree for the possession of land against B. C, B's son, murders A in consequence. The existence of the judgment is relevant, as showing motive for a crime.

(d) A is charged with theft and with having been previously convicted of theft. The previous conviction is relevant as a fact in issue.

(e) A is tried for the murder of B. The fact that B prosecuted A for libel and that A was convicted and sentenced is relevant under section 6 as showing the motive for the fact in issue.

Ingredients

i. Judgements , orders or decrees , other than those mentioned in section 34 , 35 and 36 are irrerelevant.
ii. Exception : they are relevant un following two condition

a. when the existence of some judgement , order or decree is a fact in issue
b. when they are relevant under some other provision of this act .

Anil Behari v. Latika Bala Dasi, AIR 1955 SC

A judgment in a criminal case cannot be received in a civil action to establish the truth of facts upon which it is rendered.

S. P. E. Madras v. K. V. Sundravelu, AIR 1978 SC

It was held by the Supreme Court that a previous acquittal can be cited in a fresh prosecution over the same matter, but it cannot be used to prevent a new trial.

38. Fraud or collusion in obtaining judgment, or incompetency of Court, may be proved.-Any party to a suit or other proceeding may show that any judgment, order or decree which is relevant under section 34, 35 or 36, and which has been proved by the adverse party, was delivered by a Court not competent to deliver it, or was obtained by fraud or collusion.

Ingredients

i) There are at least two parties to a suit or proceeding.

ii) One party shows a judgments, order or decree which is relevant under Section 40, 41 or 42

iii. The party proves that judgment, order or decree in the Court of law.

iv) The adverse party can show and prove

a) that the judgment was given by a Court which was incompetent, or

b) that the judgment was obtained by fraud or collusion.

Fraud

The term "fraud" is defined in section 17 of the Indian Contract Act. There must be actual or positive fraud, that is, there must be an intention to cheat or deceive another person to his injury.

'Fraud' is an extremely Collateral Act which vitiates the most solemn proceedings of Courts of Justice.

Collusion

"Collusion" means an agreement or compact between two or more persons to do some act in order to prejudice a third person, or for some improper purpose. It may be of two kinds:

1) when the facts put forward as the foundation of the sentence of the Court do not exist;

il) when they exist, but have been corruptly preconcerted for the express purpose of obtaining the sentence.

Jadu Gopal v. Panna Lal 1978 SC

A Judgment obtained by collusion means that there was no cause of action between the parties and by collusion of the parties a cause of action was feigned thus enabling the court to pass its Judgment. A Judgment obtained by fraud means one which is obtained by practising a fraud on the courts for example by suppressing facts or by obstructing the flow of evidence to the court.

Jai Narain Parasrampuria v. Pushpa Devi Saraf 2006 SC

A decree was obtained by creating Jurisdiction of the Court artificially by including a property in respect of which there was no dispute. The court held that the decree could be said to have been obtained by concealment of material facts and by a collusive and fraudulent exercise.

Asharfi Lal v. Kaili, AIR 1995 SC

Where an inference of fraud or collusion can be drawn from the negligence or gross negligence of the next friend of a minor, it would be permissible for a minor to avoid the judgment or decree passed in the earlier proceeding by invoking Section 38.

COMMENT

The comment mentioned under Section 38 of the Bharatiya Sakshya Adhiniyam, 2023 are based upon Section 44 of the Indian Evidence Act, 1872 (1 of 1872)

Under Section 44 a party can, in a collateral proceeding in which fraud may be setup as a defence. Show that a decree or order obtained by the opposite party against him was passed by a court without jurisdiction or was obtained by fraud or collusion and it is not necessary to bring an independent suit for setting it aside.

Gram Panchayat of Village Naulakha v. Ujagar Singh, (2000) 7 SCC 543.

39. Opinions of experts.—(1) When the Court has to form an opinion upon a point of foreign law or of science or art, or any other field, or as to identity of handwriting or finger impressions, the opinions upon that point of persons specially skilled in such foreign law, science or art, or any other field, or in questions as to identity of handwriting or finger impressions are relevant facts and such persons are called **experts.**

Illustrations

(a) The question is, whether the death of A was caused by poison. The opinions of experts as to the symptoms produced by the poison by which A is supposed to have died, are relevant.

(b) The question is, whether A, at the time of doing a certain act, was, by reason of unsoundness of mind, incapable of knowing the nature of the act, or that he was doing what was either wrong or contrary to law. The opinions of experts upon the question whether the symptoms exhibited by A commonly show unsoundness of mind, and whether such unsoundness of mind usually renders persons incapable of knowing the nature of the acts which they do, or of knowing that what they do is either wrong or contrary to law, are relevant.

(c) The question is, whether a certain document was written by A. Another document is produced which is proved or admitted to have been written by A. The opinions of experts on the question whether the two documents were written by the same person or by different persons, are relevant.

(2) When in a proceeding, the court has to form an opinion on any matter relating to any information transmitted or stored in any computer resource of any other electronic or digital form, the opinion of the Examiner of Electronic Evidence referred to in section 79A of the Information Technology Act, 2000 (21 of 2000), is a relevant fact.

Explanation. - For the purposes of this sub-section, an Examiner of Electronic Evidence shall be an expert.

Ingredients

i) When the Court has to form an opinion of technical matters, extraneous assistance may become necessary

ii) this section allows such assistance in the following cases iii)

iii) opinion of experts i.e. persons specially skilled in (a) foreign law; (b) science; (c) art; (d) handwriting and (e) finger impressions.

This section is an exception to the rule as regards the exclusion of opinion evidence opinions of experts are relevant upon a paint of (a) foreign law, (b) science, (c) art, (d) identity of hand writing (e) finger impressions.

Forest Range Officer v. P. Mohammed Ali, AIR 1994 SC

The Supreme Court held that expert opinion is only opinion evidence and is not helpful to the Court in interpretation of law.

Principle

It is a general rule that the opinion of witness possess in peculiar skill is admissible, whenever the subject-matter of enquiry is such that inexperienced person are unlikely to prove capable of forming a correct judgment upon it without the assistance of an expert.

Who is an Expert?

An 'expert' witness is one who has devoted time and study to a special branch of learning and thus is specially skilled on those points on which he is asked to state his opinion. His evidence on such points is admissible to enable the tribunal to come to a satisfactory conclusion. [Vide - Powell, 10*h Edition, P 39] An expert, in order to become a competent witness, need not have acquired his knowledge professionally. It is sufficient, so far as the admissibility of the evidence goes, if he has acquired special experience therein. In is the duty of the Judge to decide whether the skill of any person in the matter on which evidence of his opinion is offered, is sufficient to enable him to be considered as an expert. [Vide: Miglani v. Miglani, AIR 1979 SC)

Laxmi Chand v. Ishroo Devi, AIR 1977 SC

A handwriting expert was not in practice since 1950 and also expressed opinions beyond his natural field, his evidence was rejected.

Mahmood v. U. P., AIR 1976 SC

An expert had given no reasons in support of his opinion, nor was it shown that he possessed special skill, knowledge and experience in the science of identification of finger-prints, the Supreme Court did not consider it safe to rely upon his opinion even if it was supposed to be admissible under Section 39

Awadesh v. State of M.P., AIR 1988 SC

Expert evidence can be used to corroborate other evidence.

Foreign Law

Foreign Law is law which is not in foreign India. Expert evidence cannot be admitted where a particular law is a law of land.

Aziz Bano v. Mohammed Ibrahim Hussain (1925) ALL

It was held in the above mentioned case that, the Shia law on marriage is the law of the land and is in force in India. It cannot by no means be called foreign law nor is such law a science or art within the meaning of that Section (Section 45). It is the duty of the courts themselves to interpret the law of the land and apply it and not to depend on the opinion of witnesses howsoever learned they may be. It would be dangerous to delegate their duty to witnesses produced by either party.

Foreign law is a question of fact with which courts in India are not supposed to be conversant. Opinions of experts on foreign law are, therefore, allowed to be admitted.

Science and Art

These words include all subjects on which a course of special study or experience is necessary to the formation of an opinion. The words "science or art" are to be broadly construed, the term "science" not being limited to the higher sciences and the term "art" not being limited to fine arts but having its original sense of handicraft, trade, profession and skill in work, which, with the advance of culture, has been carried beyond the sphere of common pursuits of life into that of artistic and "scientific" action.

State v. S. J. Chaudhary, 1996 Cr. L. J. (SC)

The word "science" occurring in Section 45 includes experts in typewriters and type writing has to be read within the meaning of the word "handwriting".

Anita v.Atal Bihari, 1993 Cr. L. J. (MP)

It was held that in ascertaining date of birth, opinion of radiologist cannot be preferred over the entry in the register of births and death maintained under the provisions of an Act.

Diara Singh v. State of Punjab, AIR 1977 SC

Between the opinions of two doctors the opinion which supports direct evidence should be accepted

Ishwar Singh v. State of U.P., AIR 1976 SC

Weapons must be shown to the expert so as to enable him to comment whether all or any of the wounds would have been caused with it.

Shatrughan v. State of M.P., 1993 Cr. L. J. (M.P.)

It was held that an unexhibited report of the chemical examiner did not require to be formally proved by any witness. It was a document which proved itself under Section 293, Cr. P. C.

Handwriting

It is necessary for the admission of evidence of a handwriting expert, that the writing with which the comparison is made should be admitted and proved beyond doubt to be that of the person alleged, and that the comparison should be made in open Court in the presence of such person.

Arjun Singh v. Hazara Singh, AIR 1979 SC

Mere variation in the appearance of the signature or handwriting does not disprove the authenticity of the signature or handwriting because a fine or a stub pen, haste or deliberation, good or bad health, sitting position, drunken or sober state of a person may radically change the appearance or quality of writing.

State of Maharashtra v. Sukhdeo Singh, 1992 Cr. L. J. (SC)

The opinion of the handwriting expert being an evidence of weak quality, it needs to be corroborated and the Court has to decide in each case on merits what weight it should attach to the opinion of the expert.

Raj Mohammed v. State of H.P., 1995 Cr. L. J. (SC)

It was held that there is a natural tendency of expert to support the view of the person who calls him, hence the evidence of the Government examiner was more reliable.

Abdul Razak v. State of Maharashtra, AIR 1970 SC

The Supreme Court has expressed the opinion that in the present state of scientific knowledge evidence of dog tracking, even if admissible, is not ordinarily of much weight.

Sashi Kumar v. Subodh Kumar 1964 SC

As to the reliability of such evidence the Supreme Court laid down in quite a few cases that the evidence of an export as to handwriting is only in the nature of an opinion and it can rarely, if ever, take the place of substantive evidence. It should be corroborated either by clear direct evidence or by circumstantial evidence. Such evidence cannot be conclusive by itself. The evidence of handwriting expert unlike that of a fingerprint expert, is generally of a frail character and the court should be wary to give too much weight to it.

Ram Narain v. State of Uttar Pradesh 1973 SC

The opinion of a handwriting expert given in evidence is no less fallible than any other expert opinion adduced in evidence with the result that such evidence has to be received with great caution.

Corroboration not necessary

The Supreme Court has laid down that although the approach has to be one of caution, there is no rule of law that the evidence of an expert should of. acted upon unless substantially corroborated. **[Vide: Murarilal v. State of M.P., AIR 1980 SC]**

COMMENTS

The comments mentioned under Section 39(1) of the Bharatiya Sakshya Adhiniyam, 2023 are based upon Section 45 of the Indian Evidence Act, 1872 (1 of 1872)

Death of deceased whether due to Poisoning or strangulation - Mere statement by doctor that viscera was not preserved as there is no presence of poison not sufficient when independent panch witnesses as well as I stating that it was a case of poisoning. Non-preservation of viscera by doctor fatal to prosecution case.

Dev Kanya Tiwari v. State of U.P., AIR 2018 SC 1377.

That the uncorroborated evidence of a hand writing expert is an extremely weak type of evidence and the same should not be relied upon either for the conviction or for acquittal.

Before acting on such evidence, it is usual to see if it is corroborated either by clear direct evidence or by circumstantial evidence.

S.P.S. Rathore v. C.B.I. & Anr., AIR 2016 SC 4486.

40. Facts bearing upon opinions of experts.-Facts, not otherwise relevant, are relevant if they support or are inconsistent with the opinions of experts, when such opinions are relevant.

Illustrations

(a) The question is, whether A was poisoned by a certain poison. The fact that other persons, who were poisoned by that poison, exhibited certain symptoms which experts affirm or deny to be the symptoms of that poison, is relevant.

(b) The question is, whether an obstruction to a harbour is caused by a certain sea-wall. The fact that other harbours similarly situated in other respects, but where there were no such sea-walls, began to be obstructed at about the same time, is relevant.

Ingredients

Facts, not otherwise relevant, are relevant if they

i) supports the opinion of expert, or

ii) if they are inconsistent with the opinion of experts.

Ram Karan Mal v. State, 1990 Cr L. J.

Where the ocular evidence was that a number of assailants surrounded the person and continuously subjected him to injuries and the medical report should some knife injuries, it was held that the eye-witness account stood nullified.

Based on section 46 of Indian Evidence Act

41. Opinion as to handwriting and signature, when relevant.—(1) When the Court has to form an opinion as to the person by whom any document was written or signed, the opinion of any person acquainted with the handwriting of the person by whom it is supposed to be written or signed that it was or was not written or signed by that person, is a relevant fact.

Explanation.—A person is said to be acquainted with the handwriting of another person when he has seen that person write, or when he has received documents purporting to be written by that person in answer to documents written by himself or under his authority and addressed to that person, or when, in the ordinary course of business, documents purporting to be written by that person have been habitually submitted to him.

Illustration

The question is, whether a given letter is in the handwriting of A, a merchant in Itanagar. B is a merchant in Bengaluru, who has written letters addressed to A and received letters purporting to be written by him. C, is B's clerk whose duty it was to examine and file B's correspondence. D is B's broker, to whom B habitually submitted the letters purporting to be written by A for the purpose of advising him thereon. The opinions of B, C and D on the question whether the letter is in the handwriting of A are relevant, though neither B, C nor D ever saw A write.

(2) When the Court has to form an opinion as to the electronic signature of any person, the opinion of the Certifying Authority which has issued the Electronic Signature Certificate is a relevant fact.

Ingredients

i. The Court has to form an opinion as to the person by whom any document was written, or signed
ii. the opinion of the person acquainted with the handwriting of the person by whom a document is written or singed is relevant.

A person is said to be acquainted with the handwriting of another person

when -

a) he has to seen that person write

b) he has received documents purporting to be written by that person in answer to documents written by himself or under his authority and addressed to that person; or

c) in the ordinary course of business documents purporting to be written by that person have been habitually submitted to him.

How to Prove Handwriting

Section 41 indicates one of the methods of proving handwriting. The handwriting of a person may be proved in the following ways:

i) by the evidence of the writer himself,

ii) by the evidence of a person who has seen the person, whose writing is in

question, write,

iii) by the evidence of a person acquainted with such handwriting either by receiving letters purporting to be written by the person in answer to documents written by the witness or under his authority and addressed to that person of when in the ordinary course of business, documents purporting to be written by that person have been habitually submitted to him.

Fakhruddin v. State of Madhya Pradesh 1967 SC

Court held that handwriting may be proved by the evidence of a witness in whose presence the writing was done and this would be direct evidence and if it is available the evidence of any other kind is rendered unnecessary.

Rahim Khan v. Khurshid Ad., AIR 1975 SC

Evidence as to handwriting of a witness who did not say he was familiar with the handwriting in question was rejected.

Shankeappa v. Shushilabai, AIR 1984, Karnataka

The wife can be regarded as a person acquainted with the handwriting of her husband. A letter written by her husband to another woman acknowledging marital relationship with her was in question.

i. By the evidence of an expert in comparing handwriting . the court must satisfy by such means are open to it that the opinion may be acted upon.

ii) By the Court comparing the document in question with any others proved to the satisfaction of the Court to be genuine.

iii) The Court may also direct any person present in Court to write any words or fingers for the purpose of enabling the Court to compare the words or figure so written with any words alleged to have been written by such person.

42. Opinion as to existence of general custom or right, when relevant.—

When the Court has to form an opinion as to the existence of any general custom or right, the opinions, as to the existence of such custom or right, of persons who would be likely to know of its existence if it existed, are relevant.

Explanation.—The expression "general custom or right" includes customs or rights common to any considerable class of persons.

Illustration

The right of the villagers of a particular village to use the water of a particular well is a general right within the meaning of this section.

Daniraiji Verajlalji v. V. M. Chandraprabha, AIR 1971 Guj.

The witness in question should possess experiential qualification before his evidence gather, any credibility. It he fails in having this qualification he should show on what grounds his opinion is based. But if his opinion is not based on reliable information his mere repetition of hearsay would not carry any weight.

Ahmad Khan V. Channi Bibi, AIR 1925 PC

The Court said: The witness must be a person likely to know of the custom.

His testimony must be based upon personal knowledge. The weight of this evidence would naturally depend upon his position and character and of persons on whose statements he formed his opinion, but he cannot be confined to instances in which he had personally known the usage or custom exercised as a matter of fact.

Gururadhwaja Pd. v. S.P. Singh, 1900 Mad. LJ (PC)

The Privy Council held that the opinion of a witness as to the existence of a family custom based upon information derived from deceased persons is relevant.

Explanation - The explanation indicates that private rights are excluded from the operation of the Section. Such rights must be proved by facts such as acts of ownership. The word "general"' is an equivalent of the term "public".

43. Opinion as to usages, tenets, etc., when relevant.-When the Court has to form an opinion as to-

i) the usages and tenets of any body of men or family;

ii) the constitution and governance of any religious or charitable foundation; or

(iii) the meaning of words or terms used in particular districts or by particular classes of people,

the opinions of persons having special means of knowledge thereon, are relevant facts.

Ingredients

Opinion of persons having special means of knowledge regarding

i. usages and tenets of a body of men or family;
ii. the constitution and govemment of any religious or charitable foundation;
iii. the meaning of words or terms used in particular districts or by particular classes of people are relevant under Section 43.

Usage

These will include usages of trade and agriculture, mercantile usage and any usage common to a body of men or family. Usages of a family will include, for instance, the custom of primogeniture, or any peculiar course of descent.

Primogeniture means the fact and condition of being firstborn child; the custom of primogeniture means the right of succession belonging to firstborn child.

Tenets

This will include any opinion, principle, dogma or doctrine which is held or maintained by a body of men. It will apply to religion, politics, science, etc.

44. Opinion on relationship, when relevant.-When the Court has to form an opinion as to the relationship of one person to another, the opinion, expressed by conduct, as to the existence of such relationship, of any person who, as a member of the family or otherwise, has special means of knowledge on the subject, is a relevant fact:

Provided that such opinion shall not be sufficient to prove a marriage in proceedings under the Divorce Act, 1869 (4 of 1869), or in prosecution under sections 82 and 84 of the Bharatiya Nyaya Sanita, 2023.

Illustrations

(a) The question is, whether A and B were married. The fact that they were usually received and treated by their friends as husband and wife, is relevant.

(b) The question is, whether A was the legitimate son of B. The fact that A was always treated as such by members of the family, is relevant.

Gokal chand vs Parvin kumar (1952) SCJ

The cumulative effect of the other circumstances warrants the conclusion that the man failed to prove the factum of his marriage , with the woman , his claim to succeed to her estate as her heir under the customary law of Punjab must fail .

45. Grounds of opinion, when relevant.-Whenever the opinion of any living person is relevant, the grounds on which such opinion is based are also relevant.

Illustration

An expert may give an account of experiments performed by him for the purpose of forming his opinion .

Ingredient

i) whenever the opinion of a person is relevant.

ii) the grounds on which such opinion is based are also relevant.

Adithela Immanual Raju v. Orissa, 1992 Cr. L. J. (Orissa)

Where reasons for the support of opinion were introduced at the time of evidence, it was held that the grounds so introduced formed part of the relevant testimony, for the opposite was not thereby deprived of their opportunity to cross-examine the expert not it was otherwise prejudiced.

46. In civil cases character to prove conduct imputed, irrelevant. -In civil cases the fact that the character of any person concerned is such as to render probable or improbable any conduct imputed to him, is irrelevant, except in so far as such character appears from facts otherwise relevant.

Ingredients

i) In civil cases, no party can prove

a) that the character of the person concerned is such as to render any conduct probable

b) that the character of the person concerned is such as to render any conduct improbable.

ii) Exception: It is relevant when character is fact in issue itself.

47. In criminal cases previous good character relevant.-In criminal proceedings the fact that the person accused is of a good character, is relevant.

Ingredient

i. an accused is being tried for an offence/crime
ii. the fact that he is a person of good character
iii. is relevant .

Bhagwan swarup vs State of Maharastra AIR1965 SC

It was held by the supreme court that character evidence ; it cannot outweigh positive evidence in regard to guilt of a person.

48. Evidence of character or previous sexual experience not relevant in certain cases.-In a prosecution for an offence under section 64, section 65, section 66, section 67, section 68, section 69, section 70, section 71, section 74, section 75, section 76, section 77 or section 78 of the Bharatiya Nyaya Sanita, 2023 or for attempt to commit any such offence, where the question of consent is in issue, evidence of the character of the victim or of such person's previous sexual experience with any person shall not be relevant on the issue of such consent or the quality of consent.

Narendra Kumar vs State of NCT of Delhi 2012 SC

In prosecution for rape , unchasfity of the victim has been held to be not a determinative factor.

49. Previous bad character not relevant, except in reply.—In criminal proceedings, the fact that the accused has a bad character, is irrelevant, unless evidence has been given that he has a good character, in which case it becomes relevant.

Explanation 1.-This section does not apply to cases in which the bad character of any person is itself a fact in issue.

Explanation 2.—A previous conviction is relevant as evidence of bad character.

Ingredients

In a criminal proceedings the bad character of a person is irrelevant

Exception:

a) the evidence of bad character can be given to contradict his motion that he is a person of good character.

b) when the bad character of a person is itself fact in issue. (Explanation 1)

c) a previous conviction is relevant as evidence of bad character. (Explanation 2).

Ram Lakhan Vs U.P , AIR 1977 SC

The description of the accused as a lawbreaker amounted to evidence of character , the supreme court excluded it.

50. Character as affecting damages.-In civil cases, the fact that the character of any person is such as to affect the amount of damages which he ought to receive, is relevant.

Explanation.-In this section and sections 46, 47 and 49, the word "character" includes both reputation and disposition; but, except as provided in section 49, evidence may be given only of general reputation and general disposition, and not of particular acts by which reputation or disposition has been shown.

CHAPTER THREE

ON PROOF

51. Fact judicially noticeable need not be proved.-No fact of which the Court will take judicial notice need be proved.

Ingredients

a. no party has to prove the fact.
b. Of which the court will take judicial notice

.

52. Facts of which Court shall take judicial notice.—(1) The Court shall take judicial notice of the following facts, namely:—

(a) all laws in force in the territory of India including laws having extraterritorial operation;

(b) international treaty, agreement or convention with country or countries by India, or decisions made by India at international associations or other bodies;

(e) the course of proceeding of the Constituent Assembly of India, of Parliament of India and of the State Legislatures;

(d) the seals of all Courts and Tribunals;

(e) the seals of Courts of Admiralty and Maritime Jurisdiction, Notaries Public, and all seals which any person is authorised to use by the Constitution, or by an Act of Parliament or State Legislatures, or Regulations having the force of law in India;

(f) the accession to office, names, titles, functions, and signatures of the persons filling for the time being any public office in any State, if the fact of their appointment to such office is notified in any Official Gazette;

(g) the existence, title and national flag of every country or sovereign recognised by the Government of India;

(h) the divisions of time, the geographical divisions of the world, and public festivals, fasts and holidays notified in the Official Gazette;

(i) the territory of India;

(i) the commencement, continuance and termination of hostilities between the Government of India and any other country or body of persons;

(k) the names of the members and officers of the Court and of their deputies and subordinate officers and assistants,and also of all officers acting in execution of its process, and of advocates and other persons authorised by law to appear or act before it;

(1) the rule of the road on land or at sea.

(2) In the cases referred to in sub-section (1) and also on all matters of public history, literature, science or art, the Court may resort for its aid to appropriate books or documents of reference and if the Court is called upon by any person to take judicial notice of any fact, it may refuse to do so unless and until such person produces any such book or document as it may consider necessary to enable it to do so.

Shiv Nath V. Union of India, AIR 1965 SC

The Supreme Court held that the Court could take judicial notice of circumstances, which took place in August-September, 1947 (Communal disturbances after partition) in certain parts of the country. Under CI. (1) of this

Section the Court should take judicial notice of all Indian Laws. "Indian Law' is defined by the General Clauses Act, Section 3 (29), and includes any law, ordinance, order, byelaw, or regulation passed or made at any time by any competent legislature, authority, or person in India.

Nityanand Sharma V. State of Bihar, AIR 1966 SC

Where the Hindi version of an Act contained a wrong entry in a schedule of the Act, the Supreme Court said that the English version should be taken into judicial notice being an authoritative text of the Act.

State of Punjab v. Satya Pal, AIR 1969 SC

The Court is bound to take judicial notice of the prorogation of a State Legislative Assembly and so also the budget speech of the Finance Minister.

Onkar Nath v. Delhi Administration, AIR 1977 SC

The Court take judicial notice of the fact that an all India Railway Strike was imminent on a particular day and that it actually commenced on a certain day.

Ratan Arya v. T. N., AIR 1986 SC

The Court pointed out that the list of Section 57 is not exhaustive. The Court can also take notice of the enormous and manifold increase of rents throughout the country particularly in the urban areas.

53. Facts admitted need not be proved.-No fact needs to be proved in any proceeding which the parties thereto or their agents agree to admit at the hearing, or which, before the hearing, they agree to admit by any writing under their hands, or which by any rule of pleading in force at the time they are deemed to have admitted by their pleadings:

Provided that the Court may, in its discretion, require the facts admitted to be proved otherwise than by such admissions.

Ingredients

i. No fact need to be proved which (a) parties thereto or (b) their agents.
ii. Agree to admit by any of the following three methods:

a) they agree to admit at the hearing,
b) they agree to admit before the hearing by any writing under their hands,
C) they admit it in their pleading according to the rule for the time being in force.
iii) But the Court may require proof of the fact admitted.

Naresh Kumar v. Vishnu Kumar Nayyar, AIR 1994 Delhi

When at the initial stage of eviction proceedings, execution of agreement of tenancy showing the other party as landlord was admitted by the tenant, he subsequently could not take the plea 'that the agreement was obtained by fraud

Nagindas v. Dalpatram, AIR 1974 SC

A consent decree for possession which was based upon a compromise in a previous case and which showed the existence of a statutory ground of execution, It was held that it could take the shape of evidence or an admission which is the best proof of facts and can be made the foundation of the rights of parties.

Mahendra v. Shushila, AIR 1965 SC

In divorce case the Court does not usually decide merely on the basis of admissions in the pleadings or the petition. Whether, there is no room for supposing that parties are colluding there is no reason why admissions of parties should not be treated as evidence just as they are treated in other civil proceedings.

CHAPTER FOUR

OF ORAL EVIDENCE

54. Proof of facts by oral evidence.-All facts, except the contents of documents may be proved by oral evidence.

55. Oral evidence to be direct.—Oral evidence shall, in all cases whatever,

(i) a fact which could be seen, it must be the evidence of a witness who says he saw it;

(ii) a fact which could be heard, it must be the evidence of a witness who
says he heard it;

(iii) a fact which could be perceived by any other sense or in any other manner, it must be the evidence of a witness who says he perceived it by that sense or in that manner;

(iv) an opinion or to the grounds on which that opinion is held, it must be the evidence of the person who holds that opinion on those grounds:

Provided that the opinions of experts expressed in any treatise commonly offered for sale, and the grounds on which such opinions are held, may be proved by the production of such treatises if the author is dead or cannot be found, or has become incapable of giving evidence, or cannot be called as a witness without an amount of delay or expense which the Court regards as unreasonable:

Provided further that, if oral evidence refers to the existence or condition of any material thing other than a document, the Court may, if it thinks fit, require the production of such material thing for its inspection.

HEARSAY EVIDENCE IS AN EXCEPTION TO ORAL EVIDENCE

MEANING OF HEARSAY EVIDENCE :

Statement given by witness not upon his knowledge but upon the knowledge of someone else are called hearsay evidence .

Eg :- A is charge for killing B , X is the witness before the court states that C told me that A killed B.

Rationale Behind Exclusion of Hearsay

Derivative or second-hand evidence is excluded owing to its infirmity as composed with its original source. Thus where a witness told a material fact to another but himself resiled from it is the witness box, narration of the other was rejected as hearsay. **[Vide: Yasin Gulam Haider v. Maharashtra (1979) 4 SCC]**

Sakatar Singh v. State of Haryana 2004 SC

Hearsay evidence means the statement of a witness not based on his personal knowledge but on what he heard from others.

Kalyan Kumar Gogoi vs Ashutosh Agnihotri and others.

As the term hearsay denotes that kind of evidence which solely does not derive its value from the credit given to the witness himself but it rests in the part of competence of some other person , At the same time , it suggest the sayingof a individual and it is considered to be irrelevant and vague.

REASONS BEHIND EXCLUSION OF HEARSAY EVIDENCE

1- Witness may not give exact evidence as its not based on his knowledge

2- witness cannot be effectively cross- examined

3- there are chances of fabrication and Exaggeration

CHAPTER FIVE

OF DOCUMENTARY EVIDENCE

56. Proof of contents of documents.-The contents of documents may be proved either by primary or by secondary evidence.

Principle

The content of a document must be proved either by the production of the document which is called Primary Evidence, or by copies or oral accounts , which is called secondary.

Murarka Properties Private Ltd. Vs Beharilal Murarka , AIR 1978 SC

It was held by the supreme court that where there is documentary evidence , the oral evidence must not be given by the weight .

When a document is not required to be registered , it is a admissible , even though unregistered .

Kripa Shanker Vs Gurudas ,AIR 1995 SC

An ex- parte affidavit without affording an opportunity to the other party to test the veracity of its content by the cross – examination , cannot be a proof of its contents .

57. Primary evidence.-Primary evidence means the document itself produced for the inspection of the Court.

Explanation 1.—Where a document is executed in several parts, each part is primary evidence of the document.

Explanation 2.-Where a document is executed in counterpart, each counterpart being executed by one or some of the parties only, each counterpart is primary evidence as against the parties executing it.

Explanation 3.—Where a number of documents are all made by one uniform process, as in the case of printing, lithography or photography, each is primary evidence of the contents of the rest; but, where they are all copies of a common original, they are not primary evidence of the contents of the original.

Explanation 4.— Where an electronic or digital record is created or stored, and such storage occurs simultaneously or sequentially in multiple files, each such file is primary evidence.

Explanation 5.-Where an electronic or digital record is produced from proper custody, such electronic and digital record is primary evidence unless it is disputed.

Explanation 6.—Where a video recording is simultaneously stored in electronic form and transmitted or broadcast or transferred to another, each of the stored recordings is primary evidence.

Explanation 7.—Where an electronic or digital record is stored in multiple storage spaces in a computer resource, each such automated storage, including temporary files, is primary evidence

Illustration

A person is shown to have been in possession of a number of placards, all printed at one time from one original. Any one of the placards is primary evidence of the contents of any other, but no one of them is primary evidence of the contents of the original.

Ingredients

i. Primary evidence means the document itself produced for the inspection of the court.
ii. ii)Where a document is executed in several parts, each part is primary evidence.

iii) Where a document is executed in counter-parts, each counter-part is primary evidence as against the party executing it.

iv) Where a number of documents are made by uniform process, such as printing, lithography, or photography, each one is primary evidence of the contents of the rest.

V) Where a number of documents are made by one uniform process, but they are copies of the common original, they are not primary evidence of the contents of the original.

Comment

Based on Section 62 of Indian Evidence Act 1872. This Section defines the meaning of primary evidence which means the document itself is produced for the inspection by the Court. Where a document is executed in several parts, each part is primary evidence of the document. Where a document is executed in counter part, each counterpart is primary evidence, as against the party executing it. Where a number of documents are made by printing, lithography, or photography, each is primary evidence of the contents of the rest. Where they are copies of the common original they are not primary evidence of the contents of the original.

Kamala Rajamanikhan v. Sushila Thakur Das, AIR 1983 All.

Two wills in identical language were prepared by the process of typing in which the second copy was obtained by carbon impression. Both were duly executed and attested. Both were held to be original and not one a copy of the other. The fact that the testator inserted a remark on one of them " true copy" would not alter their character.

Primary evidence is the evidence which the law requires to be given first.

* Where a document is executed in counterpart, each counterpart is executed by one or some of the parties only, each counterpart is primary evidence as against the parties executing it, and secondary evidence as against other parties.

Prithi Chand v. State of H.P., AIR 1889 SC

A carbon copy was made by a uniform process of the certificate of a doctor (as to the condition of the rape victim) given in the performance of professional duty. It was held to be primary evidence within the meaning of the explanation to Section 57

Murarka Properties v. Beharilal Murarka 1978 SC

The court held that in the face of the documentary evidence, oral evidence is not entitled to any weight.

58. Secondary evidence.-Secondary evidence includes—

i) certified copies given under the provisions hereinafter contained;

ii) copies made from the original by mechanical processes which in themselves ensure the accuracy of the copy, and copies compared with such copies;

iii) copies made from or compared with the original;

i. counterparts of documents as against the parties who did not execute them;
ii. oral accounts of the contents of a document given by some person who has himself seen it;

(vi) oral admissions;

(vii) written admissions;

(viii) evidence of a person who has examined a document, the original of which consists of numerous accounts or other documents which cannot conveniently be examined inCourt, and who is skilled in the examination of such documents.

Illustrations

(a) A photograph of an original is secondary evidence of its contents, though the two have not been compared, if it is proved that the thing photographed was the original.

(b) A copy compared with a copy of a letter made by a copying machine is secondary evidence of the contents of the letter, if it is shown that the copy made by the copying machine was made from the original.

(c) A copy transcribed from a copy, but afterwards compared with the original, is secondary evidence; but the copy not so compared is not secondary evidence of the original, although the copy from which it was transcribed was compared with the original.

(d) Neither an oral account of a copy compared with the original, nor an oral account of a photograph or machine-copy of the original, is secondary evidence of the original.

COMMENT

The comment mentioned under Section 58 of the Bharatiya Sakshya Adhiniyam, 2023 are based upon Section 63 of the Indian Evidence Act, 1872 (1 of 1872)

Testimony of attesting witnesses self contradictory and cannot be relied upon when one of attesting witnesses deposed that will executed in presence of wife of executants but as per records, wife of executants died approximately one year ago from date of execution.

Mrs. Mary Singh & Ors. v. Padamjit Singh, AIR 2018 P&H 205.

Ram Lochan Mishra v. Pandit Harinath Mishra, (1922) Pat

In the above mentioned case a copy of a document was admitted in evidence in trial Court without objection, its admissibility cannot be challenged in the appeal Court. Because omission to object to its admissibility implies that it is a true copy and, therefore, it is not open to the Appeal Court to say whether a copy was properly compared with the original or not.

Kalyon Singh v. Chholi, AIR 1990 SC

It was held by the Supreme Court that certified copy of a registered deed is provable, but not a copy which was compared while the deed was presented for registration.

Ganesh Pd. v. Badri Pd., AIR 1980 All.

A copy of Municipal record not issued in accordance with the requirements of the Municipal act is not relevant.

Government of A.P. v. Karri Chinna Venkata Reddy, AIR 1994 SC

Copies of Copies kept in a registration office, when signed and sealed by the registering officer, are admissible for the purpose of proving the contents of the originals Letter process copies and photographs of writings are secondary evidence [Vide: Illustration (a)]. Photostatic copies of document should be accepted in evidence only after examining original records.

Mahadeva Royal v. Virabasava Royal, (1948) PC

Documents which are merely copies of copies, the originals not having been satisfactorily accounted for, are inadmissible in evidence and must be rejected.

Quamarul Islam v. S. K. Kanta, AIR 1994 SC

Newspaper reports, advertisements or messages are not admissible in evidence unless the original manuscripts are produced or they are proved by the person concerned.

Idandas v. Anant Ram Chandra, AIR 1982 SC

When a document is executed in counterpart, each party signing only the part by which he is bound, each counterpart is the best evidence against the party signing it and his privies. As to other party it is only secondary evidence. A landlords counterfoil was held to be not relevant for the purpose of showing that the arrangement was a month-to-month tenancy.

All India Anna Dravida Munnetra Kazhagam v. L.K. Tripathi 2009 SC

In a criminal proceeding for contempt, the contemner was alleged to have made a speech calculated to scandalise Judiciary in general and the order restraining a bandha in particular. The petitioner adduced evidence in the shape of Xerox copies of newspapers and tapes on the edited version of his speech telecast in T.V. No primary evidence was produced to prove the contents of the speech. The evidence produced was held to be not relevant.

Gurumukh Ram Madan v. Bhagwan Das Madan 1998 SC

Secondary evidence is allowed only in the circumstances mentioned in the Act. Any one of the ground on which secondary evidence becomes admissible would have to be proved in the first place. A certified copy of a registered document was not allowed to be proved in evidence where no account was given of the absence of the original document. The original document was such that it would naturally be in the custody of the person who was producing certified copy because it was executed in his favour.

Oral Statements [Clause 5]

Secondary evidence includes,

according to Cl. 5, oral accounts of the

contents of a document, given by some person who has himself seen the original document. But a written statement of the contents of a copy of a document, the original of which the person making the statement has not seen, cannot be accepted as secondary evidence.

* This cause does not necessarily mean that a witness who is called to give evidence as to a lost document must have himself read the document. He would be a complete witness if, having physically seen the document, the contents thereof had been read out or explained to him.

Aher Ram Goa v. Gujral, 1979 Cr. L J (DSC)

The original dying declaration was lost. A head constable who maintained a copy testified to its accuracy. This was allowed as corroborative evidence.

Vinod Chaturvedi v. State of M.P., AIR 1984 SC

Letter written by a Police Officer to his administrative superior were not allowed to be proved. The writer of the letters should have appeared in person so as to enable the opposite party to cross-examine him as to the contents of the letters.

59. Proof of documents by primary evidence.-Documents shall be proved by primary evidence except in the cases hereinafter mentioned.

P. C. Purushathama v. S. Perumal, AIR 1972 SC

It was held that once a document is properly admitted the contents of document are also admitted in evidence, though those contents may not be conclusive evidence.

J Yashoda v. K. Shobha Rani 2007 SC

Photocopies of a document, the original was with another party and therefore no chance of comparing with the original, requirement of S. 65 (a) not satisfied.

Hardip Singh v. State of Punjab 2008 SC

The fact that documents can be made falsely, a document which has been questioned has to stand the test of genuiness before it can be put to any use as the proof of a fact.

60. Cases in which secondary evidence relating to documents may be given.-Secondary evidence may be given of the existence, condition, or contents of a document in the following cases, namely: —

(a) when the original is shown or appears to be in the possession or power—

i) of the person against whom the document is sought to be proved; or

(ii) of any person out of reach of, or not subject to, the process of the

Court; or

(iii) of any person legally bound to produce it,

and when, after the notice mentioned in section 64 such person does not produce it;

(b) when the existence, condition or contents of the original have been proved to be admitted in writing by the person against whom it is proved or by his representative in interest;

(c) when the original has been destroyed or lost, or when the party offering evidence of its contents cannot, for any other reason not arising from his own default or neglect, produce it in reasonable time;

(d) when the original is of such a nature as not to be easily movable;

(e) when the original is a public document within the meaning of section

(f) when the original is a document of which a certified copy is permitted by this Adhiniyam, or by any other law in force in India to be given in evidence;

(g) when the originals consist of numerous accounts or other documents which cannot conveniently be examined in Court, and the fact to be proved is the general result of the whole collection.

Explanation.-For the purposes of—

1) clauses (a), (c) and (d), any secondary evidence of the contents of the document is admissible;

(ii) clause (b), the written admission is admissible;

(iii) clause (e) or (f), a certified copy of the document, but no other kind of secondary evidence, is admissible;

i. clause (g), evidence may be given as to the general result of the documents by any person who has examined them, and who is skilled in the examination of such document.

COMMENTS

The comments mentioned under Section 60 of the Bharatiya Sakshya Adhiniyam, 2023 are based upon Section 65 of the Indian Evidence Act, 1872 (1 of 1872)

The will registered document and the plaintiff has, prima facie, made out a case for loss of document. The plantiff had not been able to locate the same nothing more could be proved or stated by the plaintiff before which the plaintiff could be permitted to lead secondary evidence opportunity to lead secondary evidence, granted.

Sri Suru Granth Sahib Gurudwara Sri Guru Nanakpura Sahib Dhuri Pind v. Baldev Kaur & Ors., AIR 2018 Punjab & Haryana 74.

When electronic evidence is produced by party who is not in possession of device —

Such party can lead secondary evidence.

Shafhi Mohammad v. State of Himachal Pradesh, AIR 2018 SC 714.

-

61. Electronic or digital record.-Nothing in this Adhiniyam shall apply to deny the admissibility of an electronic or digital record in the evidence on the ground that it is an electronic or digital record and such record shall, subject to section 63, have the same legal effect, validity and enforceability as other document.

62. Special provisions as to evidence relating to electronic record.-The contents of electronic records may be proved in accordance with the provisions of section 63.

63. Admissibility of electronic records.—(1) Notwithstanding anything contained in this Adhiniyam, any information contained in an electronic record which is printed on paper, stored, recorded or copied in optical or magnetic media or semiconductor memory which is produced by a computer or any communication device or otherwise stored, recorded or copied in any electronic form (hereinafter referred to as the computer output) shall be deemed to be also a document, if the conditions mentioned in this section are satisfied in relation to the information and computer in question and shall be admissible in any proceedings, without further proof or production of the original, as evidence or any contents of the original or of any fact stated therein of which direct evidence would be admissible.

(2) The conditions referred to in sub-section (1) in respect of a computer output shall be the following, namely:—

(a) the computer output containing the information was produced by the computer or communication device during the period over which the computer was used regularly to create, store or process information for the purposes of any activity regularly carried on over that period by the person having lawful control over the use of the computer or communication device;

(b) during the said period, information of the kind contained in the electronic record or of the kind from which the information so contained is derived was regularly fed into the computer in the ordinary course of the said activities;

(c) throughout the material part of the said period, the computer or communication device was operating properly or, if not, then in respect of any period in which it was not operating properly or was out of operation during that part of the period, was not such as to affect the electronic record or the accuracy of its contents; and

(d) the information contained in electronic record reproduces or is derived from such information fed into the computer in the ordinary course of said activities.

(3) Where over any period, the function of creating, storing or processing information for the purposes of any activity regularly carried on over that period as mentioned in clause (a) of sub-section (2) was regularly performed by means of one or more computers or communication device, whether—

(a) in standalone mode; or

(b) on a computer system; or

(c) on a computer network; or

(d) on a computer resource enabling information creation or providing information processing and storage; or

(e) through an intermediary,

all the computers or communication devices used for that purpose during that period shall be treated for the purposes of this section as constituting a single computer or communication device; and references in this section to a computer or communication device shall be construed accordingly.

(4) In any proceeding where it is desired to give a statement in evidence by virtue of this section, a certificate doing any of the following things shall be submitted along with the electronic record at each instance where it is being submitted for admission, namely:—

(a) identifying the electronic record containing the statement and describing the manner in which it was produced;

(b) giving such particulars of any device involved in the production of that electronic record as may be appropriate for the purpose of showing that the electronic record was produced by a computer or a communication device referred to in clauses (a) to (e) of sub-section (3);

(c) dealing with any of the matters to which the conditions mentioned in sub-section (2) relate,

and purporting to be signed by a person in charge of the computer or communication device or the management of the relevant activities (whichever is appropriate) and an expert shall be evidence of any matter stated in the certificate; and for the purposes of this sub-section it shall be sufficient for a matter to be stated to the best of the knowledge and belief of the person stating it in the certificate specified in the Schedule.

(5) For the purposes of this section,—

(a) information shall be taken to be supplied to a computer or communication device if it is supplied thereto in any appropriate form and whether it is so supplied directly or (with or without human intervention) by means of any appropriate equipment;

(b) a computer output shall be taken to have been produced by a computer or communication device whether it was produced by it directly or (with or without human intervention) by means of any appropriate equipment or by other electronic means as referred to in clauses (a) to (e) of sub-section (3).

Oriental Fire & General Ins. Co. v. Chandrawali, AIR 1989 P&H

Document means a document admissible in evidence. If a document is inadmissible in consequence of not being registered or not being properly stamped, secondary evidence cannot be given of its existence.

Dropadi v. Mahagraha Bhagwat Singh, AIR 1995 Raj.

The defendant-petitioner sought to produce secondary evidence in respect of certain documents without showing his entitlement to produce it, the trial Court committed no irregularity in rejecting his application.

Effect of Refusal to Produce Document

The sole object of a notice under Section 64 to produce the original document is to enable the adversary to have the document in Court to produce it if he likes, and, if he does not, to enable the opponent to give secondary evidence thereof, so as to exclude the argument that the latter has not taken all reasonable means to produce the original which he must do before he can be permitted to make use of secondary evidence.

Muniammal v. Govindarajan, (1958) Mad.

If a person who is legally bound to produce the document refuses to produce it notwithstanding notice to do so, the existence and contents of the original document can be proved under this clause by proof of the authenticated copy.

> It any person, who is legally bound to produce the original document in the Court, does not produce it for the inspection of Court the adverse party can prove the contents of the document by producing secondary evidence. The first party will not be allowed to produce the original to contradict the secondary evidence without the consent of the opposite party or the Court.

Ashok v. Modhav Lal, AIR 1975 SC

In an election petition, the photocopy of the manuscript of a leaflet was not allowed because it was not shown where the original was. There must be some explanation as to the original.

Objection to Reception Secondary Evidence in Appeal

If a copy of document is admitted in evidence in the first Court without any objection, no objection can be allowed to be taken in Appeal as to its admissibility **[Amar Singh v. Tej Ram, AIR 1982 P & HI.**

The object of the rule is obvious, for, if the objection is taken in the first Court, the party producing the copy can ask for an adjourment in order to get the original or else to give evidence justifying the admission of secondary evidence.

64. Rules as to notice to produce.-Secondary evidence of the contents of the documents referred to in clause (a) of section 60, shall not be given unless the party proposing to give such secondary evidence has previously given to the party in whose possession or power the document is, or to his advocate or representative, such notice to produce it as is prescribed by law; and if no notice is prescribed by law, then such notice as the Court considers reasonable under the circumstances of the case:

Provided that such notice shall not be required in order to render secondary evidence admissible in any of the following cases, or in any other case in which the Court thinks fit to dispense with it: —

(a) when the document to be proved is itself a notice;

(b) when, from the nature of the case, the adverse party must know that he will be required to produce it;

(c) when it appears or is proved that the adverse party has obtained possession of the original by fraud or force;

(d) when the adverse party or his agent has the original in Court;

(e) when the adverse party or his agent has admitted the loss of the document;

(f) when the person in possession of the document is out of reach of, or not subject to, the process of the Court.

65. Proof of signature and handwriting of person alleged to have signed or written document produced.-If a document is alleged to be signed or to have been written wholly or in part by any person, the signature or the handwriting of so much of the document as is alleged to be in that person's handwriting must be proved to be in his handwriting.

66. Proof as to electronic signature.-Except in the case of a secure electronic signature, if the electronic signature of any subscriber is alleged to have been affixed to an electronic record, the fact that such electronic signature is the electronic signature of the subscriber must be proved.

67. Proof of execution of document required by law to be attested.- If a document is required by law to be attested, it shall not be used as evidence until one attesting witness at least has been called for the purpose of proving its execution, if there be an attesting witness alive, and subject to the process of the Court and capable of giving evidence:

Provided that it shall not be necessary to call an attesting witness in proof of the execution of any document, not being a will, which has been registered in accordance with the provisions of the Indian Registration Act, 1908 (16 of 1908), unless its execution by the person by whom it purports to have been executed is specifically denied.

68. Proof where no attesting witness found.—If no such attesting witness can be found, it must be proved that the attestation of one attesting witness at least is in his handwriting, and that the signature of the person executing the document is in the handwriting of that person.

COMMENT

The comment mentioned under Section 68 of the Bharatiya Sakshya Adhiniyam, 2023 are based upon Section 69 of the Indian Evidence Act, 1872 (1 of 1872)

Applicability of section 69

Propounder is not helpless when the attesting witnesses may have died, or cannot be found. Section 69 of the Evidence Act will be applicable.

Ashutosh Samanta v. Ranjan Bala Dasi, AIR 2023 SC 1422

69. Admission of execution by party to attested document.-The admission of a party to an attested document of its execution by himself shall be sufficient proof of its execution as against him, though it be a document required by law to be attested.

Badri Narayanan v. Rajabajyathammal 1996 SC

If the attesting witness denies or does not remember the execution of the document, its execution should be proved by other evidence. Section 70 so provides.

Where the attester was an illiterate person and he attested by putting his thumb impression and though it was a conveyance by his predecessor-in-interest, he was not bound by the document unless it could be shown that the document was read out to him and he understood it.

70. Proof when attesting witness denies execution.—If the attesting witness denies or does not recollect the execution of the document, its execution may be proved by other evidence.

Ram Ratan v. Bittan Kaur, AIR 1980 All

This section only operates if the attesting witness denies or does not recollect the execution of the document or has turned hostile.

Roop Lal v. Shanker, (1051) Raj.

The attestation of a document does not amount to an admission of its contents by the attesting person unless it can be proved that the document was read over to him and that he made the attestation conscious of the statement made in the document.

COMMENT

The comment mentioned under Section 70 of the Bharatiya Sakshya Adhiniyam, 2023 are based upon Section 71 of the Indian Evidence Act, 1872 (1 of 1872)

Section 71 is meant to lend assistance and come to the rescue of a party who had done his best, but driven to a state of helplessness and impassibility cannot be left down without any other means of proving due execution by "other evidence" as well.

Narayan Bhoir v. Narayan Namdeo Kadam, AIR 2003 SC 761 (SC).

71. Proof of document not required by law to be attested.-An attested document not required by law to be attested may be proved as if it was unattested.

72. Comparison of signature, writing or seal with others admitted or proved.-

(1) In order to ascertain whether a signature, writing or seal is that of the person by whom it purports to have been written or made, any signature, writing, or seal admitted or proved to the satisfaction of the Court to have been written or made by that person may be compared with the one which is to be proved, although that signature, writing or seal has not been produced or proved for any other purpose.

(2) The Court may direct any person present in Court to write any words or figures for the purpose of enabling the Court to compare the words or figures so written with any words or figures alleged to have been written by such person.

impressions.

(3) This section applies also, with any necessary modifications, to finger Impressions.

73. Proof as to verification of digital signature.-In order to ascertain whether a digital signature is that of the person by whom it purports to have been affixed, the Court may direct—

(a) that person or the Controller or the Certifying Authority to produce the Digital Signature Certificate;

(b) any other person to apply the public key listed in the Digital Signature Certificate and verify the digital signature purported to have been affixed by that person.

State of Bombay v. Kathi Kalu (1961) Bom. LR (SC)

This Section does not infringe Article 20(3) of the Indian Constitution, which provides protection against self-incrimination.

State of U.P. v. Ram Babu Misra, AIR 1980 SC

The Court can take specimen hand writing at the stage of investigation. There must be a case before it.

Sukhvinder Singh v. State of Punjab 1994 SC

It enables the court to requite the person concerned to write any words or figures to enable the court to compare them with the words or figures in question.

Bharathan v. K. Sudhakaran, AIR 1996 SC

Comparison of disputed signatures on the counter fails by the High Court Judge, without the aid of an expert or person conversant with the disputed signatures was held to be illegal.

Gaudiya Mission v. Shobha Bose 2008 SC

In this case the signature on registered will was disputed on the basis of a sale deed executed by the testator long back. The court rejected the prayer for sending the document for expert opinion. The court itself did the comparison and recorded its finding. The Supreme Court described this approach to be improper.

Public documents

74. Public and private documents.—

(1) The following documents are public documents:—

(a) documents forming the acts, or records of the acts-

1) of the sovereign authority;

ii) of official bodies and tribunals; and

iii) of public officers, legislative, judicial and executive of India or of

a foreign country;

(b) public records kept in any State or Union territory of private documents.

(2) All other documents except the documents referred to in sub-section (1) are private.

Indian Federation of S and M Newspaper Vs Press Council of India , AIR 1996 Delhi

A document furnished to the press council of India by organisations in order to substantiate their claims to recognised by the press council , are public documents are open to inspections .

COMMENT

The comment mentioned under Section 74(1) of the Bharatiya Sakshya Adhiniyam, 2023 are based upon Section 74 of the Indian Evidence Act, 1872 (1 of 1872)

Whether Copy of the chargesheet is a public document as per section 74

Copy of the chargesheet along with the necessary documents are not public documents within the definition of public documents.

Saurav Das v. Union of India, AIR 2023 SC 615.

75. Certified copies of public documents – Every public officer having the custody of a public document , which any person has right to inspect , shall give that person on demand a copy of it on payment of the legal fees therefor, together with a certificate written at the foot of such copy that it is a true copy of such document or part thereof, as the case may be, and such certificate shall be dated and subscribed by such officer with his name and his official title, and shall be sealed, whenever such officer is authorised by law to make use of a seal; and such copies so certified shall be called certified copies.

Explanation.-Any officer who, by the ordinary course of official duty, is authorised to deliver such copies, shall be deemed to have the custody of such documents within the meaning of this section.

Khadim Ali v. Jagannath, (1940) Luck.

This Section requires that a copy of a public document given by a public officer should bear a certificate written at the foot of such copy that it is true copy of such document. When a copy bears no certificate and it is not supported by the evidence of the person who prepared it, it is not admissible in evidence.

Reasons for Accepting a Certified Copy Not Original

The certified copy of a Public document is accepted but its original copy is not admissible in evidence. Its certified copy is presumed to be correct. This is an exception to the rule that primary evidence should be produced in the Court.

The main reasons are -

i) The public documents are, comparatively, not liable to corruption, alteration or misrepresentation.

ii) The whole community being interested in their preservation, in most

instances, entitled to inspect them.

iii) The number of persons interested in public documents also renders them much more frequently required for evidentiary purposes; and if the production of the originals were insisted on, not only would great inconvenience result from the same documents being wanted in different places at the same time.

iv) The handling from frequent use would soon ensure their destruction.

v) If Public documents were allowed to be taken in original, there will be great possibility that it may be lost.

Owing to above-mentioned reasons, the certified copies, which are prepared by authorised public servants, are made admissible evidence.

76. Proof of documents by production of certified copies.-Such certified copies may be produced in proof of the contents of the public documents or parts of the public documents of which they purport to be copies.

77. Proof of other official documents.—The following public documents may be proved as follows:—

(a) Acts, orders or notifications of the Central Government in any of its Ministries and Departments or of any State Government or any Department of any State Government or Union territory Administration—

(i) by the records of the Departments, certified by the head of those Departments respectively; or

(ii) by any document purporting to be printed by order of any such Government;

(b) the proceedings of Parliament or a State Legislature, by the journals of those bodies respectively, or by published Acts or abstracts, or by copies purporting to be printed by order of the Government concerned;

(c) proclamations, orders or Regulations issued by the President of India or the Governor of a State or theAdministrator or Lieutenant Governor of a Union territory, by copies or extracts contained in the Official Gazette;

(d) the Acts of the Executive or the proceedings of the Legislature of a foreign country, by journals published by their authority, or commonly received in that country as such, or by a copy certified under the seal of the country or sovereign, or by a recognition thereof in any Central Act;

(e) the proceedings of a municipal or local body in a State, by a copy of such proceedings, certified by the legal keeper thereof, or by a printed book purporting to be published by the authority of such body;

(f) public documents of any other class in a foreign country, by the original or by a copy certified by the legal keeper thereof, with a certificate under the seal of a Notary Public, or of an Indian Consul or diplomatic agent, that the copy is duly certified by the officer having the legal custody of the original, and upon proof of the character of the document according to the law of the foreign country.

Laxmi Raj Shetty vs State of T.N. 1988 SC

A newspaper is not one of the documents referred to in section 77 by which an allegation of fact can be proved.

78. Presumption as to genuineness of certified copies.—

(1) The Court shall presume to be genuine every document purporting to be a certificate, certified copy or other document, which is by law declared to be admissible as evidence of any particular fact and which purports to be duly certified by any officer of the Central Government or of a State Government:

Provided that such document is substantially in the form and purports to be executed in the manner directed by law in that behalf.

(2) The Court shall also presume that any officer by whom any such document purports to be signed or certified, held, when he signed it, the official character which he claims in such paper.

79. Presumption as to documents produced as record of evidence, etc.-Whenever any document is produced before any Court, purporting to be a record or memorandum of the evidence, or of any part of the evidence, given by a witness in a judicial proceeding or before any officer authorised by law to take such evidence or to be a statement or confession by any prisoner or accused person , taken in accordance with the law and purporting to be signed by any judge or magistrate , or by any such officer as aforesaid , the court shall presume that-

(i) the document is genuine;

(i) any statements as to the circumstances under which it was taken, purporting to be made by the person signing it, are true; and

iii) such evidence, statement or confession was duly taken.

Emperor v. Suraj Bali, (1933) All

A dying declaration, which has been recorded by a Magistrate, can be tendered in evidence without the magistrate who recorded it being called.

When a deposition is taken in open Court or a confession is taken by a magistrate, there is a degree of publicity and solemnity, which affords a sufficient guarantee for the presumption that everything was formally, correctly and honestly done.

The Emperor v. Radhe Halwai, (1902) CWN

A confession, made before a magistrate, did not bear his certificate, stating his belief that it was freely and voluntarily made. It was held that it could not be admitted under this Section without proof of its having been so made.

Ramchit Rajhbhar v. State of W. B., 1992 Cr. L. J. (Cal.)

By virtue of the provision in this section, statements recorded are presumed to be genuine, but not a guarantee of truth.

80. Presumption as to Gazettes, newspapers, and other documents.-The Court shall presume the genuineness of every document purporting to be the Official Gazette, or to be a newspaper or journal, and of every document purporting to be a document directed by any law to be keptby any person, if such document is kept substantially in the form required by law and is produced from proper custody.

Explanation.-For the purposes of this section and section 92, document is said to be in proper custody if it is in the place in which, and looked after by the person with whom such document is required to be kept; but no custody is improper if it is proved to have had a legitimate origin, or if the circumstances of the particular case are such as to render that origin probable.

Luxmi Raj Shetty v. State of T. N., AIR 1980

The presumption of genuineness attached under this Section to a newspaper cannot be treated as proof of the facts reported therein, and the statement of a fact contained in a newspaper is merely hearsay and, therefore, inadmissible in evidence.

81. Presumption as to Gazettes in electronic or digital record.-The Court shall presume the genuineness of every electronic or digital record purporting to be the Official Gazette, or purporting to be electronic or digital record directed by any law to be kept by any person, if such electronic or digital record is kept substantially in the form required by law and is produced from proper custody.

Explanation.-For the purposes of this section and section 93 electronic record are said to be in proper custody if they are in the place in which, and Looked after by the person with whom such document is required to be kept; but no custody is improper if it is prove to have had a legitimate origin , or circumstances of the particular case are such as to render that origin probable.

82. Presumption as to maps or plans made by authority of Government.-The Court shall presume that maps or plans purporting to be made by the authority of the Central Government or any State Government were so made, and are accurate; but maps or plans made for the purposes of any cause must be proved to be accurate.

COMMENT

The comment mentioned under Section 82 of the Bharatiya Sakshya Adhiniyam, 2023 are based upon Section 83 of the Indian Evidence Act, 1872 (1 of 1872)

Site plan of property of former ruler of Jodhpur was prepared and original was not produced berre High Court and no ruler on to diane os repent antence, High court

decided on the document produced. Objection of non production of original cannot be raised in Supreme Court.

Adhunik Grih Nirman Sahkari Samiti Ltd. v. State of Rajasthan, AIR 1989 SC 867.

83. Presumption as to collections of laws and reports of decisions.-The Court shall presume the genuineness of, every book purporting to be printed or published under the authority of the Government of any country, and to contain any of the laws of that country, and of every bookpurporting to contain reports of decisions of the Courts of such country.

84. Presumption as to powers-of-attorney.-The Court shall presume that every document purporting to be a power-of-attorney, and to have been executed before, and authenticated by, a Notary Public, or any Court, Judge, Magistrate, Indian Consul or Vice-Consul, or representative of the Central Government, was so executed and authenticated.

85. Presumption as to electronic agreements.-The Court shall presume that every electronic record purporting to be an agreement containing the electronic or digital signature of the parties was so concluded by affixing the electronic or digital signature of the parties.

COMMENT

The comment mentioned under Section 85 of the Bharatiya Sakshya Adhiniyam, 2023 are based upon Section 85A of the Indian Evidence Act, 1872 (1 of 1872)

Whether the second power of attorney was effective to render valid, the transaction sale and registration of the document both earlier then power of attorney. It would be so.

The second power of attorney was a valid document and it authorised the attorney to execute the document as well as present it for registration.

Jugraj Singh v. Jaswant Singh, AIR 1971 SC 761.

86. Presumption as to electronic records and electronic signatures.—(1) In any proceeding involving a secure electronic record, the Court shall presume unless contrary is proved, that the secure electronic record has not been altered since the specific point of time to which the secure status relates.

(2) In any proceeding, involving secure electronic signature, the Court shall presume unless the contrary is proved that—

(a) the secure electronic signature is affixed by subscriber with the intention of signing or approving the electronic record;

(b) except in the case of a secure electronic record or a secure electronic signature, nothing in this section shall create any presumption, relating to authenticity and integrity of the electronic record or any electronic signature.

87. Presumption as to Electronic Signature Certificates.-The Court shall presume, unless contrary is proved, that the information listed in an Electronic Signature Certificate is correct, except for information specified as subscriber information which has not been verified, if the certificate was accepted by the subscriber.

Raj Kumar Gupta v. Des Raj, AIR 1995 HP

The mere fact that the document had not been drafted or typed out by the executant before the Notary Public and the fact that the typed matter duly signed by the executant was presented before the Notary Public did not in any way make the execution and authentication doubtful.

88. Presumption as to certified copies of foreign judicial records.

(1) The Court may presume that any document purporting to be a certified copy of any judicial record of any country beyond India is genuine and accurate, if the document purports to be certified in any manner which is certified by any representative of the Central Government in or for such country to be the manner commonly in use in that country for the certification of copies of judicial records.

(2) An officer who, with respect to any territory or place outside India is a Political Agent therefor, as defined in clause (43) of section 3 of the General Clauses Act, 1897 (10 of 1897), shall, for the purposes of this section, be deemed to be a representative of the Central Government in and for the country comprising that territory or place.

89. Presumption as to books, maps and charts.- The Court may presume that any book to which it may refer for information on matters of public or general interest, and that any published map or chart, the statements of which are relevant facts, and which is produced for its inspection, was written and published by the person, and at the time and place, by whom or at which it purports to have been written or published.

90. Presumption as to electronic messages.-The Court may presume that an electronic message, forwarded by the originator through an electronic mail server to the addressee to whom the message purports to be addressed corresponds with the message as fed into his computer for **transmission;** but the Court shall not make any presumption as to the person by whom such message was sent.

District Magistrate v. G. Jothishankar, AIR 1993 SC

The detenus sent a telegram conveying that they were illegally detained but the same was not taken into consideration, it was held that a telegram is not a authentic document. It is like an unsigned/anonymous communication. Unless a telegram is confirmed by a subsequent signed application, representation or an affidavit, the contents of telegram have no authenticity at all and the same cannot be taken into consideration.

91. Presumption as to due execution, etc., of documents not produced.-The Court shall presume that every document, called for and not produced after notice to produce, was attested, stamped and executed in the manner required by law.

Kodri Smt. v. L. RS. of Fakira, AIR 1994 NOC (Raj.)

A document is shown to have remained unstamped for some time after its execution, the party who relied on it must prove that is was duly stamped.

92. Presumption as to documents thirty years old.-Where any document, purporting or proved to be thirty years old, is produced from any custody which the Court in the particular case considers proper, the Court may presume that the signature and every other part of such document, which purports to be in the handwriting of any particular person, is in that person's handwriting, and, in the case of a documentexecuted or attested, that it was duly executed and attested by the persons by whom it purports to be executed and attested.

Explanation. — The Explanation to section 80 shall also apply to this section.

Illustrations

(a) A has been in possession of landed property for a long time. He produces from his custody deeds relating to the land showing his titles to it. The custody shall be proper.

(b) A produces deeds relating to landed property of which he is the mortgagee. The mortgagor is in possession. The custody shall be proper.

(c) A, a connection of B, produces deeds relating to lands in B's possession, which were deposited with him by B for safe custody. The custody shall be proper.

COMMENTS

The comments mentioned under Section 92 of the Bharatiya Sakshya Adhiniyam, 2023 are based upon Section 90 of the Indian Evidence Act, 1872 (1 of 1872)

Proof of wills

Presumption u/s 90 as to the regularity of documents more than thirty years of age is inapplicable when it comes to proof of will.

Ashutosh Samanta v. Ranjan Bala Dasi, AIR 2023 SC 1422.

Issuance of gazette notification 32 years prior to the suit, produced and marked as evidence but no circumstance was proved, justified are inference that if might not have been published as enjoined by law, it has been held, that issue of such notification should not have been presumed leaving it to defendants to rebut that presumption.

Rohit Singh v. State of Bihar, AIR 2007 SC 10.

93- Presumption as to electronic records five years old.-Where electronic record, purporting or proved to be five years old, is produced from any custody which the Court in the particular case considers proper, the Court may presume that the electronic signature which purports to be the electronic signature of any particular person was so affixed by him or any person authorised by him in this behalf.

Explanation.-The Explanation to section 81 shall also apply to this section.

Fatima Bibi v. Irfana Begam, AIR 1980 All

The defendant produced fifty years old registered deed of gift; it was held that the burden of proving that the gift deed was fraudulent was on the plaintiff.

The presumption allowed by this section is not a presumption, which the Court is bound to make, and the Court may require the document to be proved in ordinary manner.

Mr. Taylor says- "An ancient deed, which has nothing suspicious about it, is presumed to be genuine without express proof, the witness being presumed dead, and if found in proper custody and corroborated by evidence of ancient or modern corresponding enjoyment or by other equivalent or explanatory proof, it will be presumed to have constituted part of the actual transfer of the property therein mentioned, because this is the usual course of such transfer".

Bhanwaria v. Ramratan, (1953) Raj.

The period of thirty years is to be reckoned not from the date upon which the document is filed in Court, but from the date on which, it having been tendered in evidence, Its genuineness or otherwise becomes the subject of proof.

Rangu v. Rambha, AIR 1967 Bom. L. R.

The use of word "may" indicates that the trial Court has discretion either to presume a fact as proved or to call for proof of it. The presumption is discretionary and not obligatory.

Proper Custody (Explanation)

The proper custody means the custody of any person so connected with the deed that his possession of it does not excite any suspicion of fraud. The Section insists only on a satisfactory account of the origin of the custody, and not on the history of the continuance. The provisions of the section read with the explanation insists on a satisfactory account of the origin of the possession being given by the party relying upon the documents. The custody, might not in the strictest sense legal custody, but, whether it originated in the right or wrong, the origin must be explained.

CHAPTER SIX

OF THE EXCLUSION OF ORAL EVIDENCE BY DOCUMENTARY EVIDENCE

94. Evidence of terms of contracts, grants and other dispositions of property reduced to form of document.-When the terms of a contract, or of a grant, or of any other disposition of property, have been reduced to the form of a document, and in all cases in which any matter is required by law to be reduced to the form of a document, no evidence shall be given in proof of the terms of such contract, grant or other disposition of property, or of such matter, except the document itself, or secondary evidence of its contents in cases in which secondary evidence is admissible under the provisions hereinbefore contained.

Exception 1.-When a public officer is required by law to be appointed in writing, and when it is shown that any particular person has acted as such officer, the writing by which he is appointed need not be proved.

Exception 2.—Wills admitted to probate in India may be proved by the probate.

Explanation 1.—This section applies equally to cases in which the contracts, grants or dispositions of property referred to are contained in one document, and to cases in which they are contained in more documents than one.

Explanation 2.—Where there are more originals than one, one original only needed be proved.

Explanation 3.-The statement, in any document whatever, of a fact other than the facts referred to in this section, shall not preclude the admission of oral evidence as to the same fact.

Illustrations

(a) If a contract be contained in several letters, all the letters in which it is contained

(b) If a contract is contained in a bill of exchange, the bill of exchange must be proved.

(c) If a bill of exchange is drawn in a set of three, one only need be proved.

(d) A contracts, in writing, with B, for the delivery of indigo upon certain terms.

The contract mentions the fact that B had paid A the price of other indigo contracted for verbally on another occasion. Oral evidence is offered that no payment was made for the other indigo. The evidence is admissible.

(e) A gives B a receipt for money paid by B. Oral evidence is offered of the payment.

The evidence is admissible.

Hira Devi v. Official Assignee, Bombay AIR 1958 SC

The best evidence about the contents of document is the document itself and it is the production of the document that is required by this section in proof of its contents.

95. Exclusion of evidence of oral agreement.—When the terms of any such contract, grant or other disposition of property, or any matter required by law to be reduced to the form of a document, have been proved according to section 94, no evidence of any oral agreement or statement shall be admitted, as between the parties to any such instrument or their representatives in interest, for the purpose of contradicting, varying, adding to, or subtracting from, its terms:

Provided that any fact may be proved which would invalidate any document, or which would entitle any person to any decree or order relating thereto; such as fraud, intimidation, illegality, want of due execution, want of capacity in any contracting party, want or failure of consideration, or mistake in fact or law:

Provided further that the existence of any separate oral agreement as to any matter on which a document is silent, and which is not inconsistent with its terms, may be proved. In considering whether or not this proviso applies, the

Court shall have regard to the degree of formality of the document:

Provided also that the existence of any separate oral agreement, constituting a condition precedent to theattaching of any obligation under any such contract, grant or disposition of property, may be proved:

Provided also that the existence of any distinct subsequent oral agreement to rescind or modify any such contract, grant or disposition of property, may be proved, except in cases in which such contract, grant or disposition of property is by law required to be in writing, or has been registered according to the law in force for the time being as to the registration of documents:

Provided also that any usage or custom by which incidents not expressly mentioned in any contract are usually annexed to contracts of that description, may be proved:

Provided also that the annexing of such incident would not be repugnant to, or inconsistent with, the express terms of the contract:

Provided also that any fact may be proved which shows in what manner the language of a document is related to existing facts.

Illustrations

(a) A policy of insurance is effected on goods "in ships from Kolkata to Visakhapatnam". The goods are shipped in a particular ship which is lost. The fact that particular ship was orally excepted from the policy, cannot be proved.

(b) A agrees absolutely in writing to pay B one thousand rupees on the 1st March,

2023. The fact that, at the same time, an oral agreement was made that the money should not be paid till the 31st March, 2023, cannot be proved.

(c) An estate called "the Rampur tea estate" is sold by a deed which contains a map of the property sold. The fact that land not included in the map had always been regarded as part of the estate and was meant to pass by the deed cannot be proved.

(d) A enters into a written contract with B to work certain mines, the property of B, upon certain terms. A was induced to do so by a misrepresentation of B's as to their value. This fact may be proved.

(e) A institutes a suit against B for the specific performance of a contract, and also prays that the contract may be reformed as to one of its provisions, as that provision was inserted in it by mistake. A may prove that such a mistake was made as would by law entitle him to have the contract reformed.

(f) A orders goods of B by a letter in which nothing is said as to the time of payment, and accepts the goods on delivery. B sues A for the price. A may show that the goods were supplied on credit for a term still unexpired.

(g) A sells B a horse and verbally warrants him sound. A gives B a paper in these words-"Bought of A a horse for thirty thousand rupees". B may prove the verbal warranty.

(h) A hires lodgings of B, and gives B a card on which is written-"Rooms, ten thousand rupees a month". A mayprove a verbal agreement that these terms were to include partialboard. A hires lodging of B for a year, and a regularly stamped agreement, drawn up by an advocate, is made between them. It is silent on the subject of board. A may not prove that board was included in the term verbally.

(i) A applies to B for a debt due to A by sending a receipt for the money. B keeps the receipt and does not send the money. In a suit for the amount, A may prove this.

(j) A and B make a contract in writing to take effect upon the happening of a certain contingency. The writing is left with B who sues A upon it. A may show the circumstances under which it was delivered.

Bai Hira Devi v. The Official Assignee of Bombay, 1958 SCR

Section 95 is only applicable to cases or between parties to an instrument or their representatives in interest. When the dispute is between a stranger to an instrument and a party to it or his representative in interest, this section is inapplicable, and both the stranger and the party or his representative are at liberty to lead evidence of oral agreement not withstanding the fact that such evidence, if believed, may contradict, vary, add to, or subtract from, its terms.

Chattanatha v. Central Bank of India, AIR 1965 SC

When a transaction is contained in more than one document the documents should be read and interpreted together and this section is not applicable.

T. N. Electricity Board v. N. Raju Reddiar, AIR 1996 SC

A contract was made on the basis of a tender in writing. Additional terms were not allowed to be brought in either on oral basis or by the conduct of the officers of the authority making payments on a different basis.

Niranjan Kumar v. Dhyan Singh, AIR 1976 SC

The Supreme Court allowed oral evidence to show that the real tenant was someone other than the ostensible tenant.

* There is nothing to exclude oral evidence that there was no agreement between the parties and therefore no contract.

The provisions of the Section come into force when the written instruments referred to in the section have been proved in accordance with the provisions of Section 91, that is, either by the production of the document itself or by the production of the secondary evidence of it.

Bhageshri Dayal v. Pancho, 1906 All

The rule of exclusion laid down in this section does not apply to the case of a third party who is not a party to the document. On the contrary, Section 99 distinctly provides that the person who are not parties to a document may give evidence tending to show that a contemporaneous agreement varying the terms of the document was made by them.

Naraindas v. Papammal 1967 SC

Where the parties to a promissory note payable on demand orally agreed that payment would not demanded for five years the court allowed the oral agreement to be proved.

Vishwa Nathan v. Abdul Wajib 1986 SC

It was held that section 95 precludes only the parties to the document and their representative-in-interest from giving oral evidence concerning the content of the document. Other parties are left free to give such evidence.

Tamil Nadu Electricity Board v. N. Reddiar 1996 SC

The court said that it is only when the written contract does not contain the whole of the agreement between the parties and there is any ambiguity that oral evidence is permissible to prove other conditions which also must not be inconsistent with the written contract.

Vinod Chaturvedi v. State of MP 1984 SC

Where room was allotted by writing to a doctor because he was attached to the hospital as an honorary surgeon, he was not allowed to give oral evidence that he was a lessee.

It is always permissible to look to the surrounding circumstances to see in what manner the language of a document was related to existing facts. A party is not precluded from showing that the writing was not the contract between the parties but was only a fictitious or colourable device which cloaked something else.

Kamla Devi v. Takhatmal, AIR 1964 SC

When it is said that a Court should look into all the circumstances to find an authors intention, it is only for the purpose of finding out whether the words apply accurately to the existing facts. But if the words are clear in the context of the surrounding circumstances the Court cannot rely on them to attribute to the author an intention contrary to the plain meaning of the words used in the documents.

* Fraud in order to vitiate a document must have been committed in the execution of the document i.e. a document which was not intended to be executed must have been executed. The fraud which is alleged must be such as enters into the transaction itself and enables the party to avoid the transaction. It must be fraud within the meaning of the term as used in section 1793) of the Indian Contract Act , unless and until the allegations amount to that ,there cannot be any valid plea of fraud which can be taken up by a party **(video Raghunath tiwari vs rama kant tiwari ,AIR 1991 pat.)**

96. Exclusion of evidence to explain or amend ambiguous document.-

When the language used in a document is, on its face, ambiguous or defective, evidence may not be given of facts which would show its meaning or supply its defects.

Illustrations

(a) A agrees, in writing, to sell a horse to B for "one lakh rupees or one lakh fifty thousand rupees". Evidence cannot be given to show which price was to be given.

(b) A deed contains blanks. Evidence cannot be given of facts which would show how they were meant to be filled.

Lallubhai Patel v. Lalbhai Trikumlal Mills, 1958 SCJ

The Supreme Court held that under Section 96 it is the language of the document alone that will decide the question and it would not be open to the parties or the Court to attempt to remove the vagueness by relying upon any extrinsic evidence. Such an attempt would really mean the making of a new contract between the parties.

The charges for services rendered may be recovered under Section 70 of the Indian Contract Act.

97. Exclusion of evidence against application of document to existing facts.—When language used in a document is plain in itself, and when it applies accurately to existing facts,evidence may not be given to show that it was not meant to apply to such facts.

Illustration

A sells to B, by deed, "my estate at Rampur containing one hundred bighas". A has an estate at Rampur containing one hundred bighas. Evidence may not be given of the fact that the estate meant to be sold was one situated at a different place and of a different size.

Tata Iron & Steel Co. Ltd. V. State of Bihar, AIR 1996 Pat.

When in a lease agreement with the Government, payment on interest on arrears of rent was stipulated but mode of payment was not stipulated, the collector was not prevented by Section 97 from deciding the mode.

General Coürt Martial v. Col. Aniltej Singh Phaliwal 1998 SC

It was held that section 97 comes into play only when there is a document and its language has to be considered with reference to a particular factual situation. The section applies when the execution of the document has been admitted and no vitiating factor has been proved against it. Where the document in question was a record of the proceeding of the board and contained an admission under signature of the parties, it was held that an admission could be explained by the maker of it and therefore oral evidence of explanatory nature was admissible.

COMMENT

The comment mentioned under Section 97 of the Bharatiya Sakshya Adhiniyam, 2023 are based upon Section 94 of the Indian Evidence Act, 1872 (1 of 1872)

Provision of Section 94 would apply only when execution of documents is admitted and there is no vitiating circumstances against it. Hence, oral evidence of witnesses is proceeding of Board, would be admissible in evidence.

General Court Martial v. Aniltej Singh Dhaliwal, AIR 1998 SC 983.

98. Evidence as to document unmeaning in reference to existing facts.-When language used in a document is plain in itself, but is unmeaning in reference to existing facts, evidence may be given to show that it was used in a peculiar sense.

Illustration

A sells to B, by deed, "my house in Kolkata". A had no house in Kolkata, but it appears that he had a house at Howrah, of which B had been in possession since the execution of the deed. These facts may be proved to show that the deed related to the house at Howrah.

Basavapunnareddy v. Krishnayya, AIR 1966 AP

When a sale-deed describe the land sold by wrong survey numbers, extrinsic evidence is admissible to show that the lands intended to be sold and actually sold and delivered were lands bearing different survey numbers.

99. Evidence as to application of language which can apply to one only of several persons.-When the facts are such that the language used might have been meant to apply to any one, and could not have been meant to apply to more than one, of several persons or things, evidence may be given of facts which show which of those persons or things it was intended to apply to.

Illustrations

(a) A agrees to sell to B, for one thousand rupees, "my white horse". A has two white horses. Evidence may be given of facts which show which of them was meant.

(b) A agrees to accompany B to Ramgarh. Evidence may be given of facts showing whether Ramgarh in Rajasthan or Ramgarh in Uttarakhand was meant.

100. Evidence as to application of language to one of two sets of facts, to neither of which the whole correctly applies.-When the language used applies partly to one set of existing facts, and partly to another set of existing facts, but the whole of it does not apply correctly to either, evidence may be given to show to which of the two it was meant to apply.

Illustration

A agrees to sell to B "my land at X in the occupation of Y". A has land at X, but not in the occupation of Y, and he has land in the occupation of Y but it is not at X. Evidence may be given of facts showing which he meant to sell.

101. Evidence as to meaning of illegible characters, etc.- Evidence may be given to show the meaning of illegible or not commonly intelligible characters, of foreign, obsolete, technical, local and regional expressions, of abbreviations and of words used in a peculiar sense.

Illustration

A, sculptor, agrees to sell to B, "all my mods". A has both models and modelling tools. Evidence may be given to show which he meant to sell.

State of Bihar v. Radha Krishna Singh, AIR 1983 SC

The meaning of Persian words used in a document was explained to the Judge with the help of testimonies of competent witnesses. It was held that it was proper to take the help of testimonies of competent witnesses to find out the meaning of foreign words.

102. Who may give evidence of agreement varying terms of document.-Persons who are not parties to a document, or their representatives in interest, may give evidence of any facts tending to show a contemporaneous agreement varying the terms of the document.

Illustration

A and B make a contract in writing that B shall sell A certain cotton, to be paid for on delivery. At the same time, they make an oral agreement that three months credit shall be given to A. This could not be shown as between A and B, but it might be shown by C, if it affected his interests.

103. Saving of provisions of Indian Succession Act relating to wills.-Nothing in this Chapter shall be taken to affect any of the provisions of the Indian Succession Act, 1925 (39 of 1925) as to the construction of wills.

PATENTS AND LATENT AMBIGUITIES

Meaning of Latent and Patent Ambiguities

There are two sorts of ambiguities of words - the one is ambiguitas patens and other ambiguitas latens. Patens is that which appears to be ambiguous upon the deed or instrument; latens is that which seems certain and without ambiguity, for anything that appears upon the deed or instrument; but there is some collateral matter out of the deed that breeds the ambiguity. [Vide: Best, 12" Edn. P. 211)

Norton, (S, 633, PP. 351, 352) has written, "A good test of the difference is to put the instrument into the hands of an ordinary intelligent educated person.

If, on perusal, he sees no ambiguity but there is nevertheless an uncertainty as to its application, the ambiguity is latent; if he detects the ambiguity from merely reading the instrument it is patent.

Illustrations and Comments

Illustrations

A. A agree, in writing to sell a horse to B for Rs. 1000/- or Rs. 1500/-*.

Evidence cannot be given to show which price was to be given.

COMMENT

In the above mentioned illustration the ambiguity is patent. Any ordinary person can detect the ambiguity of price whether B has to pay 1000/- rupees or 1500/- rupees, is not clear from the instrument. Extrinsic evidence cannot be given in this case.

B. A deed contains blanks, Evidence cannot be given of facts which would show how they meant to be filled.

COMMENT

The blanks in a instrument would be patent ambiguities and they could not be filled in by parole testimony as to the intention of the parties etc.

C. A sells to B, by deed, "my house in Calcutta" A had no house in Calcutta, But it appears that he has a house at Howrah, of which B had been in possession since the execution of the deed.

These facts may be proved to show that the deed related to the house of Howrah.

COMMENT

No one could detect any ambiguity from merely reading the instrument.

The ambiguity does not consist in the language, but is introduced by extrinsic circumstances. This is an illustration of latent ambiguity, Section 95, 96 and 97 deals with latent ambiguities.

The illustrations of these sections are also

examples of latent ambiguities. Extrinsic evidence can be given to explain the meaning of the documents. In fact, it is necessary to clarify the meaning of the latent ambiguitas to use these documents.

They are based on the maxim falsa demonstratio non necet (a false description does not vitiate the document.)

Extrinsic evidence of every material fact which will enable the Court to ascertain the nature and qualities of the subject - matter of the instrument, or in other words, to identify the person and things to which the instrument refers, is admissible.

CHAPTER SEVEN

OF THE BURDEN OF PROOF

104. Burden of proof.-Whoever desires any Court to give judgment as to any legal right or liability dependent on the existence of facts which he asserts must prove that those facts exist, and when a person is bound to prove the existence of any fact, it is said that the burden of proof lies on that person.

Illustrations

(a) A desires a Court to give judgment that B shall be punished for a crime which

A says B has committed. A must prove that B has committed the crime.

(b) A desires a Court to give judgment that he is entitled to certain land in the possession of B, by reason of facts which he asserts, and which B denies, to be true. A must prove the existence of those facts.

Union of India v. Mokshi Builders 1997 SC

Where a party wants a premises to be released from attachment, he must prove that the premises belonged to him and not to the judgment debtor.

Shiv Charan Singh v. Chandra Bhan, AIR 1988 SC

The party on whom the onus of proof lies must, in order to succeed, establish a prima facie case. He cannot, on failure to do so, take advantage of weakness se of his adversary's case. He must succeed by the strength of his own right and the clearness of his own proof. He cannot be heard to say that it was too difficult or virtually impossible to prove the matter in question.

Narayan v. Gopal, AIR 1960 SC

The expression "Burden of Proof' means two different things. It means sometimes that a party is required to prove an allegation before judgment can be given in its favour; it also means that on a contested issue one of the two contesting parties has to introduce evidence. The burden of proof is of importance where by reason of not discharging the burden which was put upon it, a party must eventually fail.

BURDEN OF PROOF

IN CIVIL CASES IN CRIMINAL CASES

By preponderance of evidence Beyond reasonable doubt

Raghunathi v. Raju Ramappa, AIR 1991 SC

In an eviction proceeding the fact of sub-tenancy was established and though the sub-tenant had left, the ground was not thereby wiped out, the Court said that either party was free to prove his case and all questions as to burden of proof were no longer there.

Deena v. Union of India, AIR 1983 SC

The question of burden of proof becomes irrelevant when the entire evidence on the matter is already on record.

The term "onus probandi" in its proper use, merely means that, if a fact has to be proved, the person whose interest it is to prove it, should adduce some evidence, upon which a Court could find the fact he desires the Court to find.

Gulabchand v. Kudilal, AIR 1966 SC

The Supreme Court has held that in a civil case involving allegation of charges of criminal or fraudulent character insistence on proving charges clearly and beyond reasonable doubt is wrong.

SJE Benezer v. Velayudhan 1998 SC

Where a landlord seeks eviction on the ground of bonafide personal need burden lies upon him to establish that he is genuinely in need of accommodation.

Abduller Mohammed v. State 1980 SC

It was held that there is an essential distinction between "burden of proof" and "onus of proof". Burden of proof lies on the person who has to prove a fact and it never shifts but the onus of proof shifts.

Criminal Trial

Jarnail Singh v. State of Punjab, AIR 1996 SC

It was held by the Supreme Court that in a criminal trial the burden of proving the guilt of the accused beyond all reasonable doubts always rests on the prosecution and on its failure it cannot fall back upon the evidence adducted by the accused in support of his defence to rest its case solely thereon.

State of Rajasthan v. Sher Singh, 1994 Cr. L. J. (Raj.)

In a criminal trial burden of proof squarely rests upon prosecution. Examining defence evidence first and then examining prosecution evidence is improper.

Bishandas v. Punjab, AIR 1975 SC

Recovery of articles by itself does not connect any body with the crime. Connection of the accused with the articles must be proved beyond reasonable doubt. Even total silence of the accused as to any defence on his part does not lighten, the prosecution burden to prove its case satisfactorily.

Gurucharan Singh v. State, 1993 Cr. L. J. (Bom.)

It is well established principle of law that the accused persons are under no obligation to substantiate their defence version. They are simply to come forward with a probable and plausible version.

M. P. Gupta v. Rajasthan, AIR 1974 SC

As against this heavy burden on the prosecution the accused can claim the benefit of his defence just by showing a balance of probabilities. He has not to prove his defence beyond a reasonable doubt.

BURDEN OF PROOF

IN CIVIL CASES IN CRIMINAL CASES

UPON PLAINTIFF UPON PROSECUTION

Md. Allmuddin v. State, of Assam, 1992 Cr. L. J (Gau.)

Prosecution cannot derive any advantage from falsity of the defence version , so long as it does not discharge its initial burden of proving its case beyond all reasonable doubt.

Plea of Alibi

When the accused raises the plea of alibi (his presence else where at the time of commission of the offence) burden lies on him to substantiate that fact at least to the extent of a reasonable probability. Even it the evidence produced is capable of creating a doubt whether the accused was there at the time of the happening. he becomes entitled to benefit of doubt.

Soma Bhai v. State of Gujarat, AIR 1975 SC

The Supreme Court held that it is a settled law that a plea of alibi has got to be proved to the satisfaction of the Court.

State of Maharashtra v. Narsingarao Gangaram Pimple, AIR 1984 SC

The effect of the plea of alibi must be proved with absolute certainty so as to completely exclude, the possibility of the presence of the accused at the place of occurrence.

Duch Nath Pandey v. State of U.P., AIR 1981 SC

The plea of alibi can succeed only if it is shown that the accused was so far away at the relevant time that he could not be present at the place where the crime was committed.

Niranjan Shanker Golakari v. Century Spinning and Mfg Co. Ltd.

In this case court held that where an agreement is challenged on the ground of its being a restraint of trade, the onus is upon the party supporting the contract to show that the restraint is reasonably necessary to protect his interest. Once this onus is discharged, the onus of showing that the restraint is nevertheless injurious to the public is upon the party attacking the contract.

Constitutional Validity of any enactment

In the petition challenging the constitutionality of a statute, the allegations regarding the violation of the constitutional provision should be specific, clear and unambiguous and burden of proof is on the person challenging its constitutionality [Vide: Amrit Banaspati Co. Ltd. v. Union of India, AIR 1995 SC].

In Gauri Shanker v. Union of India 1994 SC the Supreme Court stated that": i There is always a presumption in favour of constitutional validity of an enactment and the burden is upon him who attacks it to show that there has been clear transgression of the constitutional principles;

iT)

It must be presumed that the legislature understands and correctly appreciates the need of its own people, that its laws are directed to problems made manifest by experience and that its discriminations are based on adequate grounds; ili) In order to sustain the presumption of constitutionality **the** Court may take into consideration matters of common knowledge, matters of common report, the history of the times and may assume every data of facts which can be conceived existing at the time of legislation.

Matrimonial Dispute

Dastane Vs Dastane

The Supreme Court held that in matrimonial cases principles of burden of proof relating to civil cases are applicable . rules of evidence in divorce cases are same as in other civil matters , namely , decisions go by preponderance of probability . but even so the initial burden is on the petitioner.

105. On whom burden of proof lies.-The burden of proof in a suit or proceeding lies on that person who would fail if no evidence at all were given on either side.

Illustrations

(a) A sues B for land of which B is in possession, and which, as A asserts, was lett to A by the will of C, B's father. If no evidence were given on either side, B would be entitled to retain his possession. Therefore, the burden of proof is on A.

(b) A sues B for money due on a bond. The execution of the bond is admitted, but B says that it was obtained by fraud, which A denies. If no evidence were given on either side, A would succeed, as the bond is not disputed and the fraud is not proved.

Therefore, the burden of proof is on B.

Comment

The comment mentioned under Section 105 of the Bharatiya Sakshya Adhiniyam, 2023 are based upon Section 102 of the Indian Evidence Act, 1872 (1 of 1872)

The burden of proof is used in three ways (a) to indicate the duty of bringing forward evidence in support of a proposition at the beginning or later; (b) to make that of establishing a proposition as against all counter evidence; (c) an indiscriminate use in which it may mean either or both of the others.

Anil Rishi v. Gurbaksh Singh, AIR 2006 SC 1971.

Ranchod Somabhai vs Babubhai 1982

There is a essential distinction between the burden of proof of onus of proof burden of proof lies on the person who has to prove a fact and it never shifts but the Onus of proof shift. Such a shifting of onus is a continuous process in evaluation of evidence.

106. Burden of proof as to particular fact.-The burden of proof as to any particular fact lies on that person who wishes the Court to believe in its existence, unless it is provided by any law that the proof of that fact shall lie on any particular person.

Illustration

A prosecutes B for theft, and wishes the Court to believe that B admitted the theft to C. A must prove the admission. B wishes the Court to believe that, at the time in question, he was elsewhere. He must prove it.

107. Burden of proving fact to be proved to make evidence admissible.-The burden of proving any fact necessary to be proved in order to enable any person to give evidence of any other fact is on the person who wishes to give such evidence.

Illustrations

(a) A wishes to prove a dying declaration by B. A must prove B's death.

(b) A wishes to prove, by secondary evidence, the contents of a lost document. A must prove that the document has been lost.

108. Burden of proving that case of accused comes within exceptions.—

When a person is accused of any offence, the burden of proving the existence of circumstances bringing the case within any of the General Exceptions in the Bharatiya Nyaya Sanhita, 2023 or within any special exception or proviso contained in any other part of the said Sanita, or in any law defining the offence, is upon him, and the Court shall presume the absence of such circumstances.

Illustrations

(a) A, accused of murder, alleges that, by reason of unsoundness of mind, he did not know the nature of the act. The burden of proof is on A.

(b) A, accused of murder, alleges that, by grave and sudden provocation, he was deprived of the power of self-control. The burden of proof is on A.

(c) Section 117 of the Bharatiya Nyaya Sanhita, 2023 provides that whoever, except in the case provided for by sub-section (2) of section 122, voluntarily causes grievous hurt, shall be subject to certain punishments. A is charged with voluntarily causing grievous hurt under section 117. The burden of proving the circumstances bringing the case under sub-section (2) of section 122 lies on A.

109. Burden of proving fact especially within knowledge.-When any fact is especially within the knowledge of any person, the burden of proving that fact is upon him.

Illustrations

(a) When a person does an act with some intention other than that which the character and circumstances of the act suggest, the burden of proving that intention is upon him.

(b) A is charged with travelling on a railway without a ticket. The burden of proving that he had a ticket is on him.

Shah Guman Mal v. A.P., AIR 1980 SC

In the above-mentioned case, the accused was found in possession of gold with foreign markings, the Supreme Court held that the burden lay upon him to account for his possession.

COMMENTS

The comments mentioned under Section 109 of the Bharatiya Sakshya Adhiniyam, 2023 are based upon Section 106 of the Indian Evidence Act, 1872 (1 of 1872)

Applicability

a. Section 106 comes into play when the other facts have been established by the prosecution.

Dinesh Kumar v. State of Haryana, AIR 2023 SC 2795.

b. Burden to prove the guilt of the accused is always on the prosecution, however in view of Section 106 of the Evidence Act, when any fact is within the knowledge of any person, the burden of proving that fact is upon him.

Ram Gopal Mansharam v. State of Madhya Pradesh, AIR 2023 SC 1145.

Duty of Prosecution

It is the duty of prosecution to lead the primary evidence of proving its case beyond reasonable doubt but, when necessary evidence had indeed been led, the corresponding burden was heavy on the accused in terms of Section 106 of the Evidence Act to explain as to what had happened at the time of incident and as to how the death of the deceased occurred.

Prem Singh v. State of NCT of Delhi, AIR 2023 SC 193.

No proximity of time and place between last seen evidence and recovery of dead body.

Veracity of other evidence extremely doubtful; Absence of any corroboration of circumstance of "last seen together" creating reasonable doubt regarding involvement of accused. Burden of proof of fact especially within knowledge would not be shifted upon accused. Accused entitled to acquittal.

Ravi & Anr. v. State of Karnataka, AIR 2018 SC 2744.

The Evidence of the father and the brother of Bindula Devi & Ors. attendant circumstances such as strong motive the fact that the accused did not lodge any complaint about missing of Bindula Devi; that accused 6 Fudai Yadav went to the house of PW9 Debu Yadav to enquire about Bindula Devi and then suddenly deserted PWs 9 & 10 when they were going to the house of the accused, that all the accusedabsconded from their house with their belonging and that the housewas completely empty, lead to an irresistible conclusion that the accused were responsible for the death of Bindula Devi.

Joshinder Yadav v. State of Bihar, 2014 Cri, L.J. 1175 (SC).

110. Burden of proving death of person known to have been alive within thirty years.-When the question is whether a man is alive or dead, and it is shown that he was alive within thirty years, the burden of proving that he is dead is on the person who affirms it.

Surjeet Kaur v. Jhujhar Singh , AIR 1980 SC

Dealing with the facts of a case the Supreme Court observed that in view of the fact that Sardul Singh was alive on May 24, 1960, It shall be presumed that he was not dead on May 24, 1970. The appellant has alleged that Sardul Singh was dead on that date. The onus to prove that fact shall be on him.

111. Burden of proving that person is alive who has not been heard of for seven years.—When the question is whether a man is alive or dead, and it is proved that he has not been heard of for seven years by those who would naturally have heard of him if he had been alive, the burden of proving that he is alive is shifted to the person who affirms it.

Lal Chand v. Ramrup Gir, AIR 1926 PC

The Privy Council observed, "there is only one presumption, and that is that when these suits were instituted in 1916 Bhagwan Gir was no longer alive. There is no presumption at all as to the time he died. That, like any other fact, is a matter of proof".

Simultaneous Death: When two individuals perish in a common calamity (e.g. shipwreck, train collision, air crash, earthquake etc.) and the question is who died first, in the absence of evidence on the point, there is no presumption in law that the younger survived the elder. Such a question is always from first to last a pure question of fact, the onus probandi lying on the party who asserts the affirmative. **[Vide: Agha Mir Ahmed v. Mudassir Shah (1944) 71 IA 171]**

On the contrary Section 21 of the Hindu Succession Act, 1956 provides that where two persons have died in circumstances rendering it uncertain whether either of them and if so, which survived the other, then, for all purposes affecting succession to property it shall be presumed, until the contrary is proved, that the younger survived the elder.

112. Burden of proof as to relationship in the cases of partners, landlord and tenant, principal and agent.-When the question is whether persons are partners, landlord and tenant, or principal and agent, and it has been shown that they have been acting as such, the burden of proving that they do not stand, or have ceased to stand, to each other in those relationships respectively, is on the person who affirms it.

113. Burden of proof as to ownership.-When the question is whether any person is owner of anything of which he is shown to be in possession, the burden of proving that he isnot the owner is on the person who affirms that he is not the owner.

114. Proof of good faith in transactions where one party is in relation of active confidence.-Where there is a question as to the good faith of a transaction between parties, one of whom stands to the other in a position of active confidence, the burden of proving the good faith of the transaction is on the party who is in a position of active confidence.

Illustrations

(a) The good faith of a sale by a client to an advocate is in question in a suit brought by the client. The burden of proving the good faith of the transaction is on the advocate.

(b) The good faith of a sale by a son just come of age to a father is in question in a suit brought by the son. The burden of proving the good faith of the transaction is on the father.

115. Presumption as to certain offences.—(1) Where a person is accused of having committed any offence specified in sub-section (2), in—

(a) any area declared to be a disturbed area under any enactment for the time being in force, making provision for the suppression of disorder and restoration and maintenance of public order; or

(b) any area in which there has been, over a period of more than one month, extensive disturbance of the public peace,

and it is shown that such person had been at a place in such area at a time when firearms or explosives were used at or from that place to attack or resist the members of any armed forces or the forces charged with the maintenance of public order acting in the discharge of their duties, it shall be presumed, unless the contrary is shown, that such person had committed such offence.

(2) The offences referred to in sub-section (1) are the following, namely:-

(a) an offence under section 147, section 148, section 149 or section 150 of the Bharatiya Nyaya Sanhita, 2023;

(b) criminal conspiracy or attempt to commit, or abetment of, an offence under section 149 or section 150 of the Bharatiya Nyaya Sanhita, 2023.

116. Birth during marriage, conclusive proof of legitimacy.- The fact that any person was born during the continuance of a valid marriage between his mother and any man, or within two hundred and eighty days after its dissolution, the mother remaining unmarried, shall be conclusive proof that he is the legitimate child of that man, unless it can be shown that the parties to the marriage had no access to each other at any time when he could have been begotten.

S..P.S Balasubramanyam Vs Surattoyan AIR 1952 SC

A marriage presumed from a long cohabitation is also a marriage within the meaning of the section for giving rise to presumption.

This section applies to the legitimacy of children of a married person only, on the birth of a child during marriage the presumption of legitimacy is conclusive , no matter soon the birth occurs after the marriage.

The person claiming as illegitimate son must establish his alleged paternity in the same manner as any other disputed question of relationship is established.

Thakur Amjal/ V. Navab Ali Khan, 1906 PC

It is upon the person who claims to be the legitimate issue of his parents to being forward satisfactory evidence in support of their marriage.

Paternity Test

Section 116 requires the party disputing the paternity to prove non-access in order to dispel the presumption.Access

And "non-access" means the existence or non-existence of opportunity for sexual contract; it does not mean actual cohabitation. It is a rebuttable presumption of law. This presumption can only be displaced by a strong preponderance of evidence, and not by a mere balance of probabilities.

Gautam Kundu v. State of W.B., AIR 1993 SC

The Supreme Court held following rules as to permissibility of blood test to prove paternity.

i. The Courts in India cannot order blood test as a matter of course
ii. Whenever applications are made for such prayers in order to have roving inquiry, the prayer for blood test cannot be entertained.
iii. There must be a strong prima facie case in that the husband must establish non-access in order to dispel the presumption arising under Section 112
iv. The Court must carefully examine as to what would be the consequence of ordering the blood test, whether it will have the effect of branding a child as a bastard and the mother as an unchaste woman.
v. No one can be compelled to give sample of blood for analysis.

Nandlal Wasudeo Badwaik v. Lata Nandlal Badwaik 2014 SC

In this Supreme Court held that DNA test should be resorted to only if it is eminently needed and said that DNA test prevails over the presumption of conclusive proof under section 116.

117. Presumption as to abetment of suicide by a married woman.— When the question is whether the commission of suicide by a woman had been abetted by her husband or any relative of her husband and it is shown that she had committed suicide within a period of seven years from the date of her marriage and that her husband or such relative of her husband had subjected her to chu a, the out su presume, han ang teg aro ho all the other circumstanctic

of her husband.

Explanation.-For the purposes of this section, "cruelty" shall have the same meaning as in section 86 of the Bharatiya Nyaya Sanita, 2023.

Pinakin Mahipatyay Rawal v. State of Gujarat 2014 SC

It was held that the new section creates a presumption against the husband and his family. The presumption is that even if it was a case of suicide, the family must have abetted it by practising cruelly upon her. The effect of the new provision is that if some proof is available of the fact that a married woman was subjected to cruelty of her husband or his family members and she was committed suicide within seven years of her marriage the court may presume that the suicide had been abetted by her husband or his family members. This may be called presumption of abetment. The presumption will be raised by the court only after taking into account all other circumstances of the case. The necessary condition for this presumption to arise are-

1. The question before the court should be whether the commission of suicide by a married woman was the result of abetment by her husband or relatives.
2. The suicide must have taken place within a period of seven years from the date of her marriage.
3. There must be some evidence to show that her husband or his relatives had subjected her to cruelty.

COMMENT

The comment mentioned under Section 117 of the Bharatiya Sakshya Adhiniyam, 2023 are based upon Section 113A of the Indian Evidence Act, 1872 (1 of 1872)

What a court presume u/s 113A?

When the question arises as to whether commission of suicide by a woman had been abetted by her husband or any relative of her husband, and when it is shown that she had committed suicide within a period of seven years from the date of her marriage and that her husband or such relative of her husband had subjected her to cruelty, the Court can presume, having regard to the other circumstances, that such suicide has been abetted by her husband or such relative of her husband However, mere fact of commission of suicide by itself would not be sufficient for the court to raise the presumption under Section 113A of the Evidence Act, and to hold the accused guilty of Section 306 IPC.

Kashibai v. State of Karnataka, 2023 INSC 722.

118. Presumption as to dowry death.-When the question is whether a person has committed the dowry death of a woman and it is shown that soon before her death, such woman had been subjected by such person to cruelty or harassment for, or in connection with, any demand for dowry, the Court shall presume that such person had caused the dowry death.

Explanation. —For the purposes of this section, "dowry death" shall have the same meaning as in section 80 of the Bharatiya Nyaya Sanhita, 2023.

Lichama Devi v. State of Rajasthan, AIR 1988 SC

The doctor attending the injured woman testified that her neighbours brought her to the hospital and no relatives accompanied her, that she was in a serious condition and that on questioning her she told him that the mother-in-law had burnt her. This was held to be good evidence though the doctor did not record it in the medical register. Nothing could be brought in the cross-examination that he was an interested witness.

Bhola Ram v. State of U.P. 2014 SC

It was held that a mere demand for dowry is not enough for conviction the demand must be accompanied by cruelty and harassment.

State of Rajasthan v. Jaggu Ram 2008 SC

Wife died due to head injuries within one and half years of marriage, dowry harassment proved, no explanation of head injuries, cremation without informing police or parents held, husband guilty.

119. Court may presume existence of certain facts.—(1) The Court may presume the existence of any fact which it thinks likely to have happened, regard being had to the common course of natural events, human conduct and public and private business, in their relation to the facts of the particular case.

Illustrations

The Court may presume that—

(a) a man who is in possession of stolen goods soon, after the theft is either the thief or has received the goods knowing them to be stolen, unless he can account for his possession;

(b) an accomplice is unworthy of credit, unless he is corroborated in material particulars;

(c) a bill of exchange, accepted or endorsed, was accepted or endorsed for good consideration;

(d) a thing or state of things which has been shown to be in existence within a period shorter than that within which such things or state of things usually cease to exist, is still in existence;

(e) judicial and official acts have been regularly performed;

(f) the common course of business has been followed in particular cases;

(g)evidence which could be and is not produced would, if produced, be unfavourable to the person who withholds it;

(h) if a man refuses to answer a question which he is not compelled to answer by law, the answer, if given, would be unfavourable to him;

i) when a document creating an obligation is in the hands of the obligor, the obligation has been discharged.

(2) The Court shall also have regard to such facts as the following, in considering whether such maxims do or do not apply to the particular case before it:—

(i) as to Illustration (a) a shop-keeper has in his bill a marked rupee soon after it was stolen, and cannot account for its possession specifically, but is continually receiving rupees in the course of his business;

(ii) as to Illustration (b)—A, a person of the highest character, is tried for causing a man's death by an act of negligence in arranging certain machinery. B, a person of equally good character, who also took part in the arrangement, describes precisely what was done, and admits and explains the common carelessness of A and himself;

(iii) as to Illustration (b)a crime is committed by several persons. A, B and C, three of the criminals, are captured on the spot and kept apart from each other. Each gives an account of the crime implicating D, and the accounts corroborate each other in such a manner as to render previous concert highly improbable;

(iv) as to Illustration (c)—A, the drawer of a bill of exchange, was a man of business. B, the acceptor, was a young and ignorant person, completely under A's influence;

(v) as to Illustration (d)—it is proved that a river ran in a certain course five years ago, but it is known that there have been floods since that time which might change its course;

(vi) as to Illustration (e) a judicial act, the regularity of which is in question, was performed under exceptional circumstances;

(vii) as to Illustration (N-the question is, whether a letter was received. It is shown to have been posted, but the usual course of the post was interrupted by disturbances;

(viii)as to Illustration (g)—a man refuses to produce a document which would bear on a contract of small importance on which he is sued, but which might also injure the feelings and reputation of his family; (ix) as to Illustration h)—a man refuses to answer a question which he is not compelled by law to answer, but the answer to it might cause loss to him in matters unconnected with the matter in relation to which it is asked;

(x) as to Illustration (i)—a bond is in possession of the obligor, but the circumstances of the case are such that he may have stolen it.

Sodhi Transport Co. v. U.P., AIR 1986 SC

The Supreme Court held that presumption is not evidence or proof. It only shows on whom the burden of proof lies.

The effect of this rule is the make it perfectly clear that courts of justice are to use their own common sense and experience in judging the effect of particular facts, and that they are to be subject to no particular rules whatever on the subject.

Scope

This Section authorizes the Court to make certain presumptions of fact. They are all presumptions which may naturally arise, but the legislature, by the use of the word "may" instead of "shall" both in the body of the Section and in the illustrations, shows that the Court is not bound to raise them but is to consider whether in all the circumstances of the particular case they should be raised.

Presumption of Law and Presumption of Fact

Presumptions may be either of law or fact, and when of law may be either conclusive (proesumptiones juris et de jure), or rebuttable (proesumptiones juris), but when of facts (proesumptiones hominis) are always rebuttable. Mixed presumptions are those which are partly of law and partly of fact. [Vide: Phipson, 10" Edn, P. 2012)]

Presumptions of law differ from presumptions of fact as described below:

PRESUMPTIONS OF LAW

1. It derives its force from law
2. If applies to a class, the conditions of which are fixed and uniform
3. Presumptions of law are drawn by the Court, and in absence opposing evidence are conclusive for the party in whose favour they operate.
4. Presumptions of law may be either conclusive or rebuttable.
5. The Court has no discretion in respect of burden of proof.

PRESUMPTIONS OF FACT

1. It derives its force from logic
2. It applies to individual cases, the conditions which are inconsistent and fluctuating
3. Whereas presumptions of fact are of drawn by the jury, who may disregard opposing evidence however cogent.
4. Presumption of facts are always rebuttable.
5. The Court has wide power in respect of casting burden of proof on either party.

Common Course of Natural Events

The expression is appropriate in regard to such matters as the period of gestation or the continuance of life. The legitimacy of a child may have to be decided by reference to the terms during which in the ordinary course of nature gestation may continue.

State of Maharashtra v. Wasudeo, AIR 1981 SC

A Government servant was found in possession of assets disproportionate to his earnings and he was also not able to explain it, the presumption of corruption arose.

Human Conduct

All the human beings have common conduct, similar behaviour in particular circumstances. After observing common facts relating to human conduct some presumptions may be raised, for instance, when there is a long and continuous course of co-habitation between a man and woman, the law presumes in face of of tiatriage and against concubin age uade im section even in the absence of satisfactory direct evidence of marriage.

> There is a presumption that every person in his private character dogs are rightly and regularly done.

duty and unless the contrary is proved, it is presumed that all things are

State of Bihar v. P.P. Sharma 1991 SC

A presumption has to be drawn under section 114 (e) that the competent authority must have before it the necessary materials which prima facie establish the commission of the offence charged and that the competent authority had need not be set out. needed its mind before tender hate consent All the reasons tor the consent . all the reasons for the consent order need not be set out

Tulsa v. Durghatiya 2008 SC

Where after the death of her husband, a woman continued to line with another person for a long time till his death also, the court held that she had a legitimate claim over the property of the peason, as is wite. Such property could be sold by her.

Madan Mohan Singh v. Rajni Kant 2010 SC

Where a line in relationship has continued for a long time it was held that it cannot be regarded as walk in and walkout relationship because a presumption of marage would arise.

Illustrations are not Exhaustive

The illustrations given under this section are not exhaustive. They are merely a few examples of this class of "natural" presumptions, and they do not exclude the other numerous cases in which such presumptions are constantly drawn. The word used "may" indicate that the Court is not bound to draw the presumption in any particular case.

> Stolen Property Illustration (a)]

This illustration raises two presumptions viz., that person in possession of stolen goods soon after the theft is either

a) the thief, or

b) has received the goods knowing them to be stolen.

The question drawn will depend upon the circumstances and facts of each particular case. This is a presumption which the Court is not bound to draw but it is in the option of the Court to draw it. But it does not, in any way, shift the burden of proof to the accused.

Sanwat Khan v. State of Rajasthan, AIR 1956 SC

The Supreme Court held that illustration (a) to Section 114 raises merely suspicion but suspicion cannot take the place of proof.

Munshi Prasad v. State of Bihar 2001 SC

An inquest report is a part of investigation under the Criminal Procedure Code 1973, but neither the inquest report can be termed to be basic evidence or substantive evidence. Non production of such evidence or any discrepancy in it could not be regarded as fatal to the prosecution case or ever creating a suspicion about it.

State of Rajasthan v. Talevar 2011 SC

Were the stone articles were recovered from the accused on the basis of disclosure made by him and that being the only evidences against him, the court said that no presumption as to his culpability in the original crime was to be raised.

The availability of such presumption also depends upon the nature of property recovered. If the property is such that it can readily change hands, the presumption under section 114 (a) would not be available. The articles recovered were either cash, or other small things or vehicles. Such properties can easily change hands.

The accused could not be convicted merely on the basis of possession.

Lillu v. State of Haryana 2013 SC

In the matter if consent, it has been held that the medical evidence of two finger test and its interpretation violates the right of rape survivor to privacy-physical integrity and dignity. Even if the report is affirmative it cannot ipso facto give rise to presumption of consent.

*** Accomplice [Illustration (b)]**

An accomplice is one who is a guilty associate in crime. His testimonial evidence cannot be sole basis of conviction notwithstanding Section 133 of the Evidence Act, the corroboration of the accomplice's testimony is necessary.

The Bombay High Court has laid down the following four principles with regard to the nature and extent of corroboration. **[Vide: Raju v. State of Mysore, 1953 Bom. L R]**

i. that it is not necessary that there should be independent confirmation of every material particular,
ii. That independent evidence must not only make it safe to believe that the crime was committed, but in some way reasonably connect or tend to connect the accused with it by confirming in some material particular the testimony of the accomplice or complainant that the accused committed the crime
iii. That corroboration must come from independent sources, and

iv. That corroboration need not be direct evidence that the accused committed the crime - it is sufficient if it is merely circumstantial evidence of his connection with crime.

Presumption as to Consideration Illustration (c)]

The presumption on which illustration (c) is based is founded in accordance with the maxim omnia presumuntur rite esse acta i.e. all things are presumed to be done in due form.

Illustration (c) The Court may presume that the bill of exchange, accepted or endorsed, was accepted or endorsed for good consideration.

Gulab Chand v. Satya Vrat, AIR 1983 SC

The Supreme Court held that an effect of the presumption is that the plaintiff has not to produce account books to substantive consideration. The burden is upon the other party.

> Continuity of Things Illustration (d)]

This illustration is founded on the presumption which exists in favour of continuance or immutability.

Ambika Prasad v. Ram Ekbal Rai, AIR 1966 SC

If a thing or a state of things is shown to exist, an inference of its continuity within a reasonably proximate time both forwards and backwards may sometimes be drawn. The rule that the presumption of continuance may operate retrospectively also has been recognised in India. How far the presumption may be drawn backwards and forwards depends upon the nature of the things and surrounding circumstances.

*** Judicial and Official Acts [Illustration (e)]**

The rule embodies in the illustration flows from the maxim "omnia havesumenter rite et solemniter esse acts", i.e. all acts are presumed to have been rightly and regularly done.

S. R. Bommai v. Union of India, AIR 1994 SC

This illustration only means that, if an official act is proved to have been done, it will be presumed to have been regularly done, but it does not raise any presumption that an act was done for which there is no evidence and proof.

When the government accords sanction, illustration (e) of the Evidence Act raises a presumption that the official acts were regularly performed. The burden is heavier on the accused to rebut that statutory presumption. Neither motive can be presumed nor bad faith or abuse of power.

> Common Course of Business (illustration (ก)]

This illustration leaves it to the discretion of the Court to presume that a common course of business has been followed: but the Court is not bound to presume it. In commercial transactions the presumption is that the usual course of business was followed by the parties thereto.

Changamma v. State of Karnataka, AIR 1991 Cr. L. J.

When a copy of the grounds of detention was sent to the detenu but he refused to take it, the same was taken to have been served.

Harcharan Singh v. Shivrani 1981 SC

Where a notice to quit sent by registered post by a landlord to his tenant, which the latter, as verified by the postman refused to take, was presumed to have been delivered. He was also deemed to have known the contents of the letter.

With Holding of Evidence [Illustration (g)]

Illustration (g) states, " the Court may presume that evidence which could be and is not produced would, if produced, be unfavourable to the person who withhold it"...

Lakshmi Singh v. Bihar, AIR 1976 SC

The Supreme Court held that failure on the part of prosecution to explain injuries on the person of the accused can give rise to the following presumptions:

1) that the prosecution has suppressed information as to the nature of the occurrence;

2) that the witnesses who have denied those injuries are telling lies to the Court;

3) that the defence of the accused that he committed the crime in self-defence becomes more plausible shifting the burden to the prosecution.

H. D. Singh v. R.B.I., AIR 1986 SC

A worker claimed to have become permanent on account of continuous service. The Reserve Bank failed to produce any records. The worker's case was presumed to be true.

*** Refusal to Answer Questions [Illustration (h)]**

Refusal to answer a question is a legitimate ground of unfavourable inference against the person who has to answer the question under Section 148(4) of the Indian Evidence Act. But this illustration does not contemplate the case of witnesses who are not compelled to answer on grounds of privileges .

> Document in the Hands of the Obligor (Illustration (i))

This presumption is based on the natural supposition that a man will protect his own interests by securing his bond bere supposion that a man in ro. ca pro-nate is in the hands of the maker, there is a presumption that it has been paid off. If the drawee alleges that the maker come into possession of the nate unlawfully, the onus is on him to prove it.

Bhoy Hong Kong v. Ramanathan Chetty, 1902 I A

When the instrument of a debt and the security for that debt are founding the hands of the debtor, the prima facie presumption is that the debt has been discharged.

120. Presumption as to absence of consent in certain prosecution for rape.—

In a prosecution for rape under sub-section (2) of section 64 of the Bharatiya Nyaya Sanita, 2023, where sexual intercourse by the accused is proved and the question is whether it was without the consent of the woman alleged to have been raped and such woman states in her evidence before the Court that she did not consent, the Court shall presume that she did not consent.

Explanation.-In this section, "sexual intercourse" shall mean any of the acts mentioned in section 63 of the Bharatiya Nyaya Sanita, 2023.

Nawab Khan v. State, 1990 Cr. L. J (SC)

This section comes into play on proof by the prosecution that sexual intercourse had, in fact, taken place and on the victim girl saying before the Court that there was no consent on her part.

Rafiq v. State of U.P., AIR 1981 SC

The Supreme Court held that the absence of marks of injury on the accused is not fatal in each case, nor does the absence of such physical injuries on the-prosecutor warrant the presumption of consent on her part.

CHAPTER EIGHT

ESTOPPEL

121. Estoppel.-When one person has, by his declaration, act or omission, intentionally caused or permitted another person to believe a thing to be true and to act upon such belief, neither he nor his representative shall be allowed, in any suit or proceeding between himself and such person or his representative, to deny the truth of that thing.

Illustration

A intentionally and falsely leads B to believe that certain land belongs to A, and thereby induces B to buy and pay for it. The land afterwards becomes the property of A, and A seeks to set aside the sale on the ground that, at the time of the sale, he had no title. He must not be allowed to prove his want of title.

Pickard Vs Sears 1837

The doctrine of estoppel is based upon the law laid down in Pickard vs sears . in this case it was held that where a person "by the words or conduct wilfully causes another to believe the existence of a certain state of things and induces him to act on that belief , so as to alter his own previous positions , the former is concluded from averring against the latter a different state of things as existing at the same time.

Banwari Lal vs. Sukhdarshan, AIR 1973 SC

It was held by the Supreme Court that:

a. The doctrine embodied in the Section is not a rule of equity but a rule of evidence formulated and applied in courts of law.

b) It precludes a person from denying the truth of some statement previously made by himself.

C) No cause of action arises upon estoppel itself.

Allegans contraria non est audiendus

The estoppel is based on the above mentioned maxim which means - a person alleging contradictory facts should not be heard. This Latin maxim is the species of presumptio juris et de jure, where the fact presumed is taken to be true, not as against all the world, but against a particular party, and that only by reason of some act done.

Estoppel applies not only in favour of the person induced to change his position but of a transferee from such person and it binds not only the persons whose representations or actions have created it, but all persons claiming under or through him by gratuitous title.

Estoppel is a rule of civil action. It has no application to criminal proceedings, though in such proceedings it would be prejudicial to set up a different story.

Estoppel and Presumption

ESTOPPEL

1. An estoppel is a personal disqualification laid upon a person peculiarly circumstanced from proving particular fact.

2. Estoppel is the species of presumption where the fact presumed is taken to be true, not as against all the world, but as against a particular party, and that only by reason of some act done.

3. It is a rule of civil law.

4. Estoppel is a rule of Evidence Act.

PRESUMPTION

1. Whereas a presumption is a rule that particular inferences shall be drawn from particular facts.
2. It applies against the whole world.
3. Presumption applies in civil as well as in criminal law.
4. It is also a rule of Evidence Act.

Estoppel and Admission

ESTOPPEL

1.Estoppel binds only parties and privies thereto.

2- Estoppel being a rule of evidence , an action cannot be founded on it.

3- it applies in civil law

ADMISSION

1. It is not with admission. Even stranger can take advantage of admission .
2. An action can be founded on an admission
3. Same applicability in civil law .

Estoppel and Res Judicata

(Res judicata is defined under section 11 of CPC).

ESTOPPEL

1. Estoppel is part of the law of evidence and proceeds upon the equitable principle of altered situation.
2. Estoppel prohibits a party from proving anything which contradicts the previous declaration or acts to the prejudice of a party who , relying upon them , altered his position.
3. Estoppel shuts the mouth of a party.

RES JUDICATA

1. While Res judicata belongs to procedure and is based on the principle that there must be an end to litigation.
2. Res judicata prohibits the court from enquiring into a matter already adjudicated.

ESTOPPEL AND WAIVERs not a cause of action . it may assist

Estoppel and waiver are different . Estoppel is not a cause of action . it may assist

122. Estoppel of tenant and of licensee of person in possession.-No tenant of immovable property, or person claiming through such tenant, shall, during the continuance of the tenancy or any time thereafter, be permitted to deny that the landlord of such tenant had, at the beginning of the tenancy, a title to such immovable property; and no person who came upon any immovable property by the licence of the person in possession thereof shall be permitted to deny that such person had a title to such possession at the time when such licence was given.

COMMENT

The comment mentioned under Section 122 of the Bharatiya Sakshya Adhiniyam, 2023 are based upon Section 116 of the Indian Evidence Act, 1872 (1 of 1872)

A person who comes upon any immovable property by the licence of the person in possession thereof, shall not be permitted to deny that such person had title to such possession at the time when such licence was given.

Bansraj Lalta Prasad Mishra v. Stanley Parker Jones, 2006(3) SCC 91.

123. Estoppel of acceptor of bill of exchange, bailee or licensee.-No acceptor of a bill of exchange shall be permitted to deny that the drawer had authority to draw such bill or to endorse it; nor shall any bailee or licensee be permitted to deny that his bailor or licensor had, at the time when the bailment or licence commenced, authority to make such bailment or grant such licence.

Explanation 1.— The acceptor of a bill of exchange may deny that the bill was really drawn by the person by whom it purports to have been drawn.

Explanation 2.—If a bailee delivers the goods bailed to a person other than the bailor, he may prove that such person had a right to them as against the bailor.

CHAPTER NINE

OF WITNESSES

124. Who may testify.-All persons shall be competent to testify unless the Court considers that they are prevented from understanding the questions put to them, or from giving rational answers to those questions, by tender years, extreme old age, disease, whether of body or mind, or any other cause of the same kind.

Explanation.—A person of unsound mind is not incompetent to testify, unless he is prevented by his unsoundness of mind from understanding the questions put to him and giving rational answers to them.

The competency of witness:

The competency of a witness to testify as a witness is a condition precedent to the administration to him of an oath or affirmation, and is a question distinct from that of his credibility when he has been sworn or has been affirmed.

Child Witness

No age is fixed for a competent child witness. The intellectual capacity of a child to understand questions and to give rational answers thereto is the sole test of his testimonial competency and not any particular age. **[Santosh Roy vs.**

State of W.B. 1992 Cr. L.J. (Cal.)]

In Suresh Kumar vs. State of U.P., AIR 1981 SC, the Supreme Court accepted the evidence of a child of five years who was the sole witness to murder by a domestic servant.

S.G. Mahite vs. Maharashtra, AIR 1973 SC

In the above mentioned case, the only witness in the field was a teenage girl and she was found on facts to be truthful, the court held that such evidence must be scrutinised with care.

Rameshwar Kalyan Singh vs. State of Rajasthan, AIR 1952 SC

The Supreme Court said that it is always desirable that the courts should always record their opinion that the child understands the duty of speako muce truth, otherwise the credibility of the witness may be seriously affected, so much So, that in some cases, it may be necessary to reject the evidence altogether.

Prakash vs. State of M.P., AIR 1993 SC

The child witness aged 14 years was the victim's younger brother and gave proper account of the incident of murder witnessed by him. It was held that his testimony could not be discarded on the ground of likelihood of his being tutored.

Lunatic

The explanation to Section 124 applies to the case of a monomaniac or person afflicted with partial insanity. Such person will be an admissible witness if the Judge finds him upon investigation capable of understanding the subject in respect of which he is required to testify. [Hill's Case (1851)]

Accused witness

An accused person is competent to testify within this Section, but before the amendment of the Criminal Procedure Code in 1956 he was incompetent to be a witness, for an oath could not be administered to him and without it, no witness can be lawfully examined, or give evidence, by or before a court.

Partisan Witness

An interested witness means a person who wants to see that the accused gets convicted because of his own animus or otherwise.

Tata Singh vs. State of Punjab, AIR 1987 SC

The fact that a witness is related to one of the parties cannot by itself be considered sufficient to warrant discarding of his evidence in toto. But the evidence of such witness should be scrutinised carefully.

Unchaste woman

State of Maharashtra vs. Madhukar N. Mardikar (1991) 1 SCC

The Supreme Court held that even an unchaste woman may be a competent witness and the judgment can be based upon her testimony.

In the above mentioned case, the Supreme Court stated, "Even a woman of easy virtue is entitled to privacy and no one can invade her privacy as and when he likes. She is entitled to protect her person if there is an attempt to violate it against her wish. She is equally entitled to the protection of law. Therefore, merely because she is a woman of easy virtue, her evidence cannot be thrown overboard. At the most the officer called upon to evaluate her evidence would be required to administer caution unto himself before accepting her evidence."

Falsus in uno, Falsus in omnibus

The maxim "falsus in uno, falsus in omnibus" means false in one thing false in everything.

Ugar Ahir vs. The State of Bihar, AIR 1965 SC

The Supreme Court held that false in one thing false in everything is neither a rule of law nor a rule of practice, for the reason that hardly one comes across a witness whose evidence does not contain a grain of untruth or, at any rate, exaggeration or embellishment. But it is the duty of the court to scrutinise the evidence carefully and separate the grain from the chaff.

125. Witness unable to communicate verbally.—A witness who is unable to speak may give his evidence in any other manner in which he can make it intelligible, as by writing or by signs; but such writing must be written and the signs made in open Court and evidence so given shall be deemed to be oral evidence. Provided that if the witness is unable to communicate verbally, the Court shall take the assistance of an interpreter or a special educator in recording the statement , and such statement shall be Videographed .

Kishan Singh vs. Stat of Rajasthan, 1995 Cr. L.., Rajasthan

A witness having become dumb was physically incapable to give his statement, it was held that no adverse inference could be drawn against the prosecution in not examining him.

126. Competency of husband and wife as witnesses in certain cases.

1) In all civil proceedings the parties to the suit, and the husband or wife of any party to the suit, shall be competent witnesses.

2) In criminal proceedings against any person , the husband or wife of such person , respectively , shall be a competent witness.

Bhanwar Lal Vaid vs. Bhanwar Lal Agarwal, 1951 Raj 1

The Rajasthan High Court held that parties in civil proceedings are competent witnesses and, therefore, their testimony is to be scrutinised in the same manner as that of any other witness. There is no inflexible rule that if a party gives his testimony he must be disbelieved because he is a party to the suit.

In Aidan vs. State of Rajasthan, 1993 Cr.L.J. Raj,

it was held that the truthfulness of the statement of wife could not be disbelieved merely because the emotional reaction was different from what it should have been in the opinion of the court.

127. Judges and Magistrates. — No Judge or Magistrate shall, except upon the special order of some Court to which he is subordinate, be compelled to answer any question as to his own conduct in Court as such Judge or Magistrate, or as to anything which came to his knowledge in Court as such Judge or Magistrate; but he may be examined as to other matters which occurred in his presence whilst he was so acting.

Illustrations

(a) A, on his trial before the Court of Session, says that a deposition was improperly taken by B, the Magistrate. B cannot be compelled to answer questions as to this, except upon the special order of a superior Court.

(b) A is accused before the Court of Session of having given false evidence before B, a Magistrate. B cannot be asked what A said, except upon the special order of the superior Court.

(c) A is accused before the Court of Session of attempting to murder a police officer whilst on his trial before B, a Sessions Judge. B may be examined as to what occurred.

COMMENT

The comment mentioned under Section 127 of the Bharatiya Sakshya Adhiniyam, 2023 are based upon Section 121 of the Indian Evidence Act, 1872 (1 of 1872)

The Court must realize that its process should be used sparingly and after careful deliberation, if the arbitratorshould be brought into witness-box. In no case he can be summoned merely to show how he arrived at conclusion.

Union of India v. Orient Engg. & Commercial Co. Ltd. AIR 1977 SC 2445.

128. Communications during marriage.—No person who is or has been married, shall be compelled to disclose any communication made to him during marriage by any person to whom he is or has been married; nor shall he be permitted to disclose any such communication, unless the person who made it, or his representative in interest, consents, except in suits between married persons, or proceedings in which one married person is prosecuted for any crime committed against the other.

Shankar vs. State of T.N., 1994 Cr.L.J.

The accused confessed his offence to his mistress, it was held that Section 128 did not in any way stop her from giving evidence in the court of law.

Ram Bharosey v. State of U.P. 1954 SC

The accused was on trial for murdering his neighbour. His wife was summoned as a witness. She stated that her husband told her that he would give her ornaments. She then asked him where he had gone so early in the morning and he replied that he had gone to the middle house (the house where the deceased lived) to get them. This conversation was held to be irrelevant under section 128

.

129. Evidence as to affairs of State.-No one shall be permitted to give any evidence derived from unpublished official records relating to any affairs of State, except with the permission of the officer at the head of the department concerned, who shall give or withhold such permission as he thinks fit.

State of Punjab vs. S.S. Singh, AIR 1961 SC

The Supreme Court indicated that interests other than the interest of the public do not masquerade in the garb of public interest and take undue advantage of the provisions of this section. Subject to this reservation the maxim salus populi est suprema lex which means that regard for public welfare is the highest law, is the basis of the provision contained in this Section.

It is for the court to decide whether a document falls within the category "unpublished official records relating to any affairs of State."

The approach to this question has now acquired new dimensions particularly since the decision of a bench of seven Supreme Court Judges in **S.P. Gupta vs. Union of India, AIR 1982 SC.** The case arose out of the matter of the transfer of a High Court Judge and the non-renewal of the term of an additional Judge. The correspondence between the law Minister and the Chief Justice of the High Court and the State Goverment was required to be produced. It was held that though the "advice" was protected from judicial scrutiny by virtue of Article 74 of the Constitution, the material on the basis of which the advice was formulated was not protected.

R. Ramanna vs. State, AIR 1971 AP 196

The High Court in exercise of its powers under Article 226 of the Constitution of India can call for scrutiny and perusal by it unpublished official records. In so doing the court is not permitted to allow anybody to give any evidence from these records relating to any affairs of State within the meaning of this Section.

S.R. Bommai vs. Union of India, AIR 1994 SC

The Supreme Court held that privilege under Section 129 can be claimed in respect of ministerial advice tendered to the President of India.

Production without claim of privilege

Chaudhary v. Governor of Bihar, AIR 1980 SC

The Supreme Court held that notwithstanding the bar contained in Article 163(3) of the Constitution it shall be the sole discretion of the Governor concerned to produce the proceedings of the Council of Minister without any objection and without any claim of privilege before any court of law and then there is nothing to debar the court from taking into the same. This proposition of law was affirmed by the Apex Court in Chaudhary's case (AIR 1980 SC) overruling the judgment of Patna High Court in Ram Nagina v. Sahni (AIR 1976 Pat.)

R.K. Jain v. Union of India, AIR 1993 SC

The oath of secrecy does not absolve the Minister from filing affidavit stating grounds or reasons in support of his claim for public interest immunity.

130. Official communications.-No public officer shall be compelled to disclose communication made to him in official confidence, when he considers that the public interests would suffer by the disclosure.

King-Emperor v. Bhagwati Prasad (1929) 5 Luck

If communications are not made in official confidence, they cannot be regarded as privileged e.g. statement made to a stationmaster of a railway in the course of an inquiry of a theft by some railway employees.

131. Information as to commission of offences.-No Magistrate or police officer shall be compelled to say when he got any information as to the commission of any offence, and no revenue officer shall be compelled to say public revenue.

Explanation.-"revenue officer" means any officer employed in or about the business of any branch of the public revenue.

132. Professional communications.—(1) No advocate, shall at any time be permitted, unless with his client's express consent, to disclose any communication made to him in the course and for the purpose of his service as such advocate, by or on behalf of his client, or to state the contents or condition of any document with which he has become acquainted in the course and for the purpose of hisprofessional service, orto disclose any advice given by him to his client in the course and for the purpose of such service:

Provided that nothing in this section shall protect from disclosure of—

(a) any such communication made in furtherance of any illegal purpose;

(b) any fact observed by any advocate, in the course of his service as such, showing that any crime or fraud has been committed since the commencement of his service.

(2) It is immaterial whether the attention of such advocate referred to in the proviso to sub-section (1), was or was not directed to such fact by or on behalf of his client.

Explanation.-The obligation stated in this section continues after the professional service has ceased.

Illustrations

(a) A, a client, says to B, an advocate-"I have committed forgery, and I wish you to defend me". As the defence of a man known to be guilty is not a criminal purpose, this communication is protected from disclosure.

(b) A, a client, says to B, an advocate-"I wish to obtain possession of property by the use of a forged deed on which I request you to sue". This communication, being made in furtherance of a criminal purpose, is not protected from disclosure.

(c) A, being charged with embezzlement, retains B, an advocate, to defend him. In the course of the proceedings, B observes that an entry has been made in A's account book, charging A with the sum said to have been embezzled, which entry was not in the book at the commencement of his professional service. This being a fact observed by B in the course of his service, showing that a fraud has been committed since the commencement of the proceedings, it is not protected from disclosure.

(3) The provisions of this section shall apply to interpreters, and the clerks or employees of advocates.

Daya Shankar Dubey vs. Subhash Kumar 1992 Cr.L.J. (All)

It was held by Allahabad High Court that no privilege can be claimed in respect of a document which came into the possession of the opposite party and has been filed in the court, though it might contain legal advice.

- The rule is: "once privileged always privileged". The explanation to this Section clearly shows this.

In re an Attorney (1924) 26 Bom LR (FB)

It was decided by the Federal Bench that if an attorney discloses the facts which came to his knowledge while he was engaged as an attorney he will be guilty of professional misconduct.

- There is no privilege to communications made before the creation of relationship of pleader and client.

133. Privilege not waived by volunteering evidence.—If any party to a suit gives evidence therein at his own instance or otherwise, he shall not be deemed to have consentedthereby to such disclosure as is mentioned in section 132; and, if any party to a suit or proceeding calls any such advocate, as a witness, he shall be deemed to have consented to such disclosure only if he questions such advocate, on matters which, but for such question, he would not be at liberty to disclose.

134. Confidential communication with legal advisers.—No one shall be compelled to disclose to the Court any confidential communication which has taken place between him and his legal adviser, unless he offers himself as a witness, in which case he may be compelled to disclose any such communications as may appear to the Court necessary to be known in order to explain any evidence which he has given, but no others.

Privileged document falling into hands of third persons

A diversion of views can be seen on this topic -

Calcraft vs. Guest (1898) 1 QB, 759

It was held that once a document subject to legal privilege has fallen into the hands of a third person, the privilege no longer attaches to it and it may be adduced in evidence.

Lord Ashburton vs. Pope (1913) 2 Ch 469

It was held that whose privileged document falls into the hands of a stranger may obtain an injunction for the return of the document and restrain the stranger from their use in any legal proceedings.

Goddard vs. Nationwide Building Society (1986) 1 All ER

Nourse J. explained, "The crucial point is that the party who desires the protection must seek it before the other party has adduced the confidential communication in evidence or otherwise relied on it at trial."

Conclusion

The conclusion of the different views described in the above mentioned three cases may be found in a famous case:

Guinness Peat Properties Ltd. vs. Fitzroy Robinson Partnership, 1987 2 All ER

The court observed that the courts would normally give such relief if disclosure was obtained by fraud or trick and added that if the document had come to the possession of the other side due to mistake or carelessness on the part of the party entitled to the document or by his advisers, the balance will be very different from the balance in a fraud case.

135. Production of title-deeds of witness not a party.-No witness who is not a party to a suit shall be compelled to produce his title-deeds to any property, or any document in virtue of which he holds any property as pledgee or mortgagee or any document the production of which might tend to criminate him, unless he has agreed in writing to produce them with the person seeking the production of such deeds or some person through whom he claims.

136. Production of documents or electronic records which another person, having possession, could refuse to produce.-No one shall be compelled to produce documents in his possession or electronic records under his control, which any other person would be entitled to refuse to produce if they were in his possession or control, unless such last-mentioned person consents to their production.

137. Witness not excused from answering on ground that answer will criminate.—A witness shall not be excused from answering any question as to any matter relevant to the matter in issue in any suit or in any civil or criminal proceeding, upon the ground that the answer to such question will criminate, or may tend directly or indirectly to criminate, such witness, or that it will expose, or tend directly or indirectly to expose, such witness to a penalty or forfeiture of any kind:

Provided that no such answer, which a witness shall be compelled to give, shall subject him to any arrest or prosecution, or be proved against him in any criminal proceeding, except a prosecution forgiving false evidence by such answer.

138 Accomplice.-An accomplice shall be a competent witness against an accused person; and a conviction is not illegal if it proceeds upon the corroborated testimony of an accomplice.

(Accomplice is a person who participates in the commission of actual crime charged against an accused .)

Evidentiary value of testimony of Accomplice

1. When an Accomplice makes a testimony it is not seen as reliable evidence for a conviction , and it has to be verified with other material evidence called corroboration.
2. The reason behind not considering the evidence provided by the accomplice is to protect himself as he may go against the co accused , but this does not mean that court cannot rely on the evidence of accomplice .
3. An accomplice shall be a competent witness as against the accused person and conviction of accused based on the testimony of accomplice is valid even though it is not corroborated in material particular.

Sheikh Zakir v. State of Bihar 1983 SC

The court said "if a conviction is based on the evidence of a prosecutrix without any corroboration, it will not be illegal on that sole ground. But in the case of a grown-up or married woman, it is always safe to insist on corroboration, which can be sought from either direct or circumstantial evidence or both".

Dinesh v. State of Rajasthan 2008 SC

Court held that victim of rape is not an accomplice. Corroboration is not the sine qua non for conviction in a rape case to insist upon corroboration in the Indian setting amounts to adding insult to injury.

139. Number of witnesses.—No particular number of witnesses shall in any case be required for the proof of any fact.

COMMENT

The comment mentioned under Section 139 of the Bharatiya Sakshya Adhiniyam, 2023 are based upon Section 134 of the Indian Evidence Act, 1872 (1 of 1872)

Number of witness

Evidence has to be weighed and not counted. In other words, it is the quality of evidence that matters and not the quantity.

Munna Lal v. State of Uttar Pradesh, AIR 2023 SC 634.

CHAPTER TEN

OF EXAMINATION OF WITNESSES

140. Order of production and examination of witnesses.-The order in which witnesses are produced and examined shall be regulated by the law and practice for the time being relating to civil and criminal procedure respectively, and, in the absence of any such law, by the discretion of the Court.

141. Judge to decide as to admissibility of evidence.— (1) When either party proposes to give evidence of any fact, the Judge may ask the party proposing to give the evidence in what manner the alleged fact, if proved, would be relevant; and the Judge shall admit the evidence if he thinks that the fact, if proved, would be relevant, and not otherwise.

(2) If the fact proposed to be proved is one of which evidence is admissible only upon proof of some other fact, such last mentioned fact must be proved before evidence is given of the fact first mentioned, unless the party undertakes to give proof of such fact, and the Court is satisfied with such undertaking.

(3) If the relevancy of one alleged fact depends upon another alleged fact being first proved, the Judge may, in his discretion, either permit evidence of the first fact to be given before the second fact is proved, or require evidence to be given of the second fact before evidence is given of the first fact.

Illustrations

(a) It is proposed to prove a statement about a relevant fact by a person alleged to be dead, which statement is relevant under section 26. The fact that the person is dead must be proved by the person proposing to prove the statement, before evidence is given of the statement.

(b) It is proposed to prove, by a copy, the contents of a document said to be lost.

The fact that the original is lost must be proved by the person proposing to produce the copy, before the copy is produced.

(c) A is accused of receiving stolen property knowing it to have been stolen. It is proposed to prove that he denied the possession of the property. The relevancy of the denial depends on the identity of the property. The Court may, in its discretion, either require the property to be identified before the denial of the possession is proved, or permit the denial of the possession to be proved before the property is identified.

(d) It is proposed to prove a fact A which is said to have been the cause or effect of a fact in issue. There are several intermediate facts B, C and D which must be shown to exist before the fact A can be regarded as the cause or effect of the fact in issue. The Court may either permit A to be proved before B, C or D is proved, or may require proof of B, C and D before permitting proof of A.

Munir Ad Vs State of Rajasthan , AIR 1989 SC

The Supreme Court upheld the rejection of the evidence of a living person by means of an affidavit . the proper course was for the signatory of the affidavit to appear in person .

142. Examination of witnesses._(1) The examination of a witness by the party who calls him shall be called his examination-in-chief.

(2) The examination of a witness by the adverse party shall be called his cross-examination.

(3) The examination of a witness, subsequent to the cross-examination, by the party who called him, shall be called his re-examination.

Chandan v. State of Rajasthan, AIR 1988 SC

When the opportunity to the opposite party of cross-examination was not given, the evidence is liable to be rejected as hearsay evidence.

State of Karnataka v. S. Dhandapani Modatiar

It was held that some time should intervene between framing of the charge and statement of the accused about his desire of cross-examination because in a large number of cases they are ignorant of the law and must need advice before they can make up mind whether to further cross-examine the witness already examined by the prosecution.

Tej Prakash v. State of Haryana, 1996 SC

Where a witness was not examined in examination-in-chief, tendering him for cross-examination is not permissible.

143. Order of examinations.—(1) Witnesses shall be first examined-in-chief, then (if the adverse party so desires) cross-examined, then (if the party calling him so desires) re-examined.

(2) The examinations in chief and cross-examination must relate to relevant facts, but the cross-examination need not be confined to the facts to which the witness testified on his examination-in-chief.

(3) The re-examination shall be directed to the explanation of matters referred to in cross-examination; and, if new matter is, by permission of the Court, introduced in re-examination, the adverse party may further cross-examine upon that matter.

Examination-in-Chief

This will ordinarily be in the form of a connected narrative, brought out by question put to the witness by the party calling him. It must relate to relevant facts . No leading question can be asked .

Unless evidence of reputation be admissible, witnesses, must, in general merely speak to facts within their own knowledge, and they will not be permitted to express their own belief or opinion. [Taylor, 12" Edition]

A prominent law writer Taylor has said, "on some particular subjects, positive and direct testimony may often be unattainable, and, in such cases, a witness is allowed to testify to his belief or opinion, or even to draw inferences respecting the fact in question from other facts, provided these last facts be within his personal knowledge."

This mode of examination chiefly prevails on questions of science or trade, where from the difficulty of obtaining more direct and positive evidence, persons of skill, sometime called experts, are allowed, not to testify the facts, but to give their opinions in evidence.

Gopal Saran v. Satyanarayana, AIR 1989 SC

It was held that the statement made in examination-in-chief, lose much of their credibility and weight unless they are put into the crucible of cross-examination and emerge unscathed from the test.

Cross-Examination

The testimony of a witness is not legal evidence unless it is subject to cross-examination and where no opportunity has been given to the appellant's counsel to test the veracity of the principle prosecution witness, the evidence of such a witness is not legal testimony and cannot be the basis of a judicial pronouncement. **[Ganesh Yadav v. State of Assam, 1995 Cr. L. J (Gua.)]**

Juwar Singh v. State of M.P., AIR 1981 SC

The objects of cross-examination are to impeach the accuracy, credibility and general value of the evidence given in chief; to shift the facts already stated by the witness, to detect and expose discrepancies, or to elicit suppressed facts which will support the case of the cross-examining party.

Rules For Cross-Examination

i. Cross-examination must related to relevant facts but unlike re-examined, it need not be confined to facts depose ant in She preceding examination . Further it differs from both of them inasmuch as leading
ii. No cross-examination can be allowed of a witness who is "summoned to produce a document but it is competent of a witness to character .
iii. A witness may be cross examined as to precious statements made by him in writing or reduced into witing and or reduced into writing and relevant to matter in question without such writing being shown to him or being proved .

iv. iv) The range of cross-examination is unlimited, the only circumscribing limits being that it must relate to relevant facts .

v) the legislature has tried to give very wide powers to the cross examiner to help him in finding out the truth in oral depositions laid out before the court. In cross-examination, a witness may be asked question.

a) to test his veracity;

b) to discover who he is and what is his position in life;

c) to shake his credit by injuring his character, although his answer might criminate him or expose him to penalty or forfeiture .

vi) All questions or inquires which are indecent or scandalous, unless they relate to facts in issue, are to beavoided ; so alsoall questions which are calculated to insult or annoy or couched in a needlessly offensive form .

vii) Cross-Examination is in almost all cases undertaken by the adverse party; but the court may permit a party to cross-examine his own witness if he proves to be a hostile witness .

viii) In criminal cases (Warrant cases) tried by magistrates, the accused person can after the charge has been framed and he has given his plea, re-call and cross-examine any witness for the prosecution .

Muniappan v. State of Madras, AIR 1961 SC

An accused is entitled in law to put further questions to a prosecution witness by way of cross-examination in respect of what he had stated in reply to questions put to him in cross-examination by the other co-accused.

Re-Examination

The object of re-examination is to afford the party calling a witness an opportunity of filing in the lacuna or explaining the inconsistencies which the cross-examination has discovered in the examination-in-chief of the witness. It accordingly limited to the explanation of matters referred to in cross-examination . It partakes of the nature of examination-in-chief in as much as no leading questions can be asked .

Mir Mohammed Omar v. State of West Bengal, AIR 1989 SC

If a question has been omitted in the examination-in-chief, and cannot in strictness, be asked on a re-examination as not arising out of cross-examination, it is usual for the counsel to request the Judge to make inquiry and such a request is generally granted.

Examination by Court

It is not the province of the court to examine the witnesses, unless the pleaders on either side have omitted to put some material question or questions.

Ram Chander v. Haryana, AIR 1981 SC

The Supreme Court held that Judge is right to question is circumscribed by the adverse system. Where the Judge rebuked a witness and threatened him with prosecution for perjury, the whole trial was held to be vitiated'.

144. Cross-examination of person called to produce a document.-A person summoned to produce a document does not become a witness by the mere fact that he produces it, and cannot be cross-examined unless and until he is called as a witness.

COMMENT

The comment mentioned under Section 144 of the Bharatiya Sakshya Adhiniyam, 2023 are based upon Section 139 of the Indian Evidence Act, 1872 (1 of 1872)

That the appellant had an opportunity to cross-examination PW3 and PW4 on all the so-called contradictions to the two witnesses but he failed to avail of this opportunity by not cross-examining PW3 and PW4. On the other hand, the appellant adopted the cross-examination to these two witnesses.

In this view of the matter; he cannot now be permitted to find fault in the evidence of PW3 and PW4 and rely upon some contradictions which otherwise do not show any contradiction much less major one affecting their testimony.

Bilal Hajar alias Abdul Hameed v. State Rep. by Inspector of Police, AIR 2018 SC 4780.

145. Witnesses to character.-Witnesses to character may be cross-examined and re-examined.

146. Leading questions.—(1) Any question suggesting the answer which the person putting it wishes or expects to receive, is called a leading question.

(2) Leading questions must not, if objected to by the adverse party, be asked in an examination-in-chief, or in a re-examination, except with the permission of the Court.

(3) The Court shall permit leading questions as to matters which are introductory or undisputed, or which have, in its opinion, been already sufficiently proved.

(4) Leading questions may be asked in cross-examination.

Varkey joseph Vs State of Kerala AIR 1993 SC

The prosecution cannot put leading question on the material part of the evidence which the witness intends to give against the accused . such leading questions offend the right of the accused to fair trial enshrined in Article 21 of the Constitution. It is not a curable irregularity.

147. Evidence as to matters in writing.—Any witness may be asked, while under examination, whether any contract, grant or other disposition of property, as to which he is giving evidence, was not contained in a document, and if he says that it was, or if he is about to make any statement as to the contents of any document, which, in the opinion of the Court, ought to be produced, the adverse party may object to such evidence being given until such document is produced, or until facts have been proved which entitle the party who called the witness to give secondary evidence ofit.

Explanation. —A witness may give oral evidence of statements made by other persons about the contents of documents if such statements are in themselves relevant facts.

Illustration

The question is, whether A assaulted B. C deposes that he heard A say to D-"B wrote a letter accusing me of theft, and I will be revenged on him". This statement is relevant, as showing A's motive for the assault, and evidence may be given of it, though no other evidence is given about the letter.

148. Cross-examination as to previous statements in writing.—A witness may be cross-examined as to previous statements made by him in writing or reduced into writing, and relevant to matters in question, without such writing being shown to him, or being proved; but, if it is intended to contradict him by the writing, his attention must, before the writing can be proved, be called to those parts of it which are to be used for the purpose of contradicting him.

COMMENT

The comment mentioned under Section 148 of the Bharatiya Sakshya Adhiniyam, 2023 are based upon Section 145 of the Indian Evidence Act, 1872 (1 of 1872)

Cross-examination sought, in case of Judge Loya's death, of persons whose statements have been recorded at time of incident. Persons whose statement have been recorded not witness in proceedings for seeking court mandated injury. No matter of right to cross-examine judicial officers and doctor in such proceedings arise. Application for cross-examination, cannot be allowed.

Tehseen Poonawalla v. Union of India & Anr., AIR 2018 SC 5538.

Merely because the defence witnesses have not been contradicted by reference to their previous statements following the provisions of section 145 of the Evidence Act would not permit the court to accept the version as unfolded by the said witnesses to be the correct.

Balakrishnan & Ors. v. State of Tamil Nadu, AIR 2018 SC 1153.

149. Questions lawful in cross-examination.-When a witness is cross-examined, he may, in addition to the questions hereinbefore referred to, be asked any questions which tend—

(a) to test his veracity; or

(b) to discover who he is and what is his position in life; or

(c) to shake his credit, by injuring his character, although the answer to such questions might tend directly or indirectly to criminate him, or might expose or tend directly or indirectly to expose him to a penalty or forfeiture:

Provided that in a prosecution for an offence under section 64, section 65, section 66, section 67, section 68, section 69, section 70 or section 71 of the Bharatiya Nyaya Sanita, 2023 or for attempt to commit any such offence, where the question of consent is an issue, it shall not be permissible to adduce evidence or to put questions in the cross-examination of the victim as to the general immoral character, or previous sexual experience, of such victim with any person for proving such consent or the quality of consent.

State vs Hazura singh , (1952) Patiala

When the cross examination of a witness before a committing magistrate was deferred to the conclusion of the examination – in – chief of the witness but the witness breathed his last before the date fixed in the case and could not be cross examined , it was held that it could not be said that the accused was given opportunity to cross – examinethe witness and had failed to avoid of the opportunity therefore the statement of such a witness could not be received in evidence at the trial .

150. When witness to be compelled to answer.—If any such question relates to a matter relevant to the suit or proceeding, the provisions of section 137 shall

amply thereto.

151. Court to decide when question shall be asked and when witness compelled to answer.—(1) If any such question relates to a matter not relevant to the suit or proceeding, except in so far as it affects the credit of the witness by injuring his character, the Court shall decide whether or not the witness shall be compelled to answer it, and may, if it thinks fit, warn the witness that he is not obliged to answer it.

2) In exercising its discretion, the Court shall have regard to the following considerations, namely:—

(a) such questions are proper if they are of such a nature that the truth of the imputation conveyed by them would seriously affect the opinion of the Court as to the credibility of the witness on the matter to which he testifies;

(b) such questions are improper if the imputation which they convey relates to matters so remote in time, or of such a character, that the truth of the imputation would not affect, or would affect in a slight degree, the opinion of the Court as to the credibility of the witness on the matter to which he testifies;

(c) such questions are improper if there is a great disproportion between the importance of the imputation made against the witness's character and the importance of his evidence;

(d) the Court may, if it sees fit, draw, from the witness's refusal to answer, the inference that the answer if given would be unfavourable.

The Queen vs Holmes (1871) LR

Justice Kelley C.B. observed ." on an indictment for rape , or attempts to rape , or for an indecent assault , the prosecutrix cannot be asked in cross -examination whether she had connection with another person not the accused and if she denies it , evidence cannot be called to contradict her.

152. Question not to be asked without reasonable grounds.-No such question as is referred to in section 151 ought to be asked, unless the person asking it has reasonable grounds for thinking that the imputation which it conveys is well-founded.

Illustrations

(a) An advocate is instructed by another advocate that an important witness is a dacoit. This is a reasonable ground for asking the witness whether he is a dacoit.

(b) An advocate is informed by a person in Court that an important witness is a dacoit. The informant, on being questioned by the advocate, gives satisfactory reasons for his statement. This is a reasonable ground for asking the witness whether he is a dacoit.

(c) A witness, of whom nothing whatever is known, is asked at random whether he is a dacoit. There are here no reasonable grounds for the question.

(d) A witness, of whom nothing whatever is known, being questioned as to his mode of life and means of living, gives unsatisfactory answers. This may be a reasonable ground for asking him if he is a dacoit.

153. Procedure of Court in case of question being asked without reasonable grounds.—-If the Court is of opinion that any such question was asked without reasonable grounds, it may, if it was asked by any advocate, report the circumstances of the case to the High Court or other authority to which such advocate is subject in the exercise of his profession.

154. Indecent and scandalous questions.-The Court may forbid any questions or inquiries which it regards as indecent or scandalous, although such questions or inquiries may have some bearing on the questions before the

Court, unless they relate to facts in issue, or to matters necessary to be known in order to determine whether or not the facts in issue existed.

155. Questions intended to insult or annoy.— The Court shall forbid any question which appears to it to be intended to insult or annoy, or which, though proper in itself, appears to the Court needlessly offensive in form.

156. Exclusion of evidence to contradict answers to questions testing veracity.—When a witness has been asked and has answered any question which is relevant to the inquiry only in so far as it tends to shake his credit by injuring his character, no evidence shall be given to contradict him; but, if he answers falsely, he may afterwards be charged with giving false evidence.

Exception 1.-If a witness is asked whether he has been previously convicted of any crime and denies it, evidence may be given of his previous conviction.

Exception 2.-If a witness is asked any question tending to impeach his impartiality, and answers it by denying the facts suggested, he may be contradicted.

Illustrations

(a) A claim against an underwriter is resisted on the ground of fraud. The claimant is asked whether, in a former transaction, he had not made a fraudulent claim. He denies it.

Evidence is offered to show that he did make such a claim. The evidence is inadmissible.

(b) A witness is asked whether he was not dismissed from a situation for dishonesty.

He denies it. Evidence is offered to show that he was dismissed for dishonesty. The evidence is not admissible.

(c) A affirms that on a certain day he saw B at Goa. A is asked whether he himself was not on that day at Varanasi. He denies it. Evidence is offered to show that A was on that dayat Varanasi. The evidence is admissible, not as contradicting A on a fact which affects his credit, but as contradicting the alleged fact that B was seen on the day in question in Goa. In each of these cases, the witness might, if his denial was false, be charged with giving false evidence.

(d) A is asked whether his family has not had a blood feud with the family of B against whom he gives evidence. He denies it. He may be contradicted on the ground that the question tends to impeach his impartiality.

Attorney General v. Hitchcock, (1847) 1 Ex 91

The Section is based on the above mentioned decision of Pollock, C. B. he observed in the above mentioned case, a witness may be contradicted as to anything he denies having said provided it be connected with the issue as a matter capable of being distinctly given in evidence, or it must be so far connected with it as to be a matter which, if answered in a particular way would contradict a part of the witness's testimony; and if it is neither the one nor the other of these, it is collateral to, though in some sense it may be considered as connected with, the subject of inquiry. A distinction should be observed between those matters which may be given in evidence by way of contradiction, as directly affecting the story of the witness touching the issue before the jury, and those matters which affect the motives, temper and character of the witness, not with respect to his credit, but with reference to his feeling towards one party or the other."

State of Karnataka v. R. Yarappa Reddy 2000 SC

Where there was a loan transaction between the accused and the husband of the eye-witness and that affected the impartiality of the eye-witness and yet no questions were asked to her about the transaction, her evidence was not allowed to be contradicted by citing the statements of other witnesses about the transaction.

157. Question by party to his own witness.— (1) The Court may, in its discretion, permit the person who calls a witness to put any question to him which might be put in cross-examination by the adverse party.

2) Nothing in this section shall disentitle the person so permitted under sub-section (1), to rely on any part of the evidence of such witness.

(**Hostile Witness** :- A Hostile Witness is one who from the manner in which he gives the evidence shows that he is not desirous of telling truth to the court)

Shatrughan v. State of M.P., 1993 Cr. L.J. (MP)

It was held by the MP High Court that a hostile witness is not necessarily a false witness. Merely because one part of the statement of a witness was not favourable to the party calling him, the Court shoute not readily conclude that noe was suppressing the truth or that his testimony was adverse to that party. Hostility of a witness is to be Judge from the answers given by him.

Dahyabhai v. State of Gujarat, AIR 1964 SC

The Court can permit a person, who calls a witness, to put questions to him which might be put in the cross-examination at any state of the examination of the examine him on the answers elicited which do not find place in examination-in-chief.

Meena Gopalkrishna Mudiliyar v. State of Maharashtra, AIR 1993 SC

Where the party calling a witness declared him hostile and allowed to be cross-examined. It was held that he was not necessarily unreliable witness and his evidence, if corroborated by other reliable evidence, can sustain conviction.

Gulshan Kumar v. State 1993 Cr. L. J

It was held by the Supreme Court that the court is not preculated from taking into account the statement of a hostile witness altogether and it is not necessary to discard the same in toto. Thus, the statement of a hostile witness can be relied upon partly.

Partisan Witness

A partisan witness is a person who favours one party due to his personal interests i.e. blood relation, family blood-feud, monetary interests, relationship by blood or by marriage etc. In the case of evidence of a partisan witness no conviction can be bases on his evidence unless it is corroborated in material particulars.

Bhanuprasad v. State of Gujarat (1968) Bombay L. R. 43 SC

The Supreme Court held that it is not illegal to convict an accused on the testimony of a partisan witness but it may be appropriate to look for reliable corroboration.

Bhupender Singh v. State of Punjab, AIR 1968 SC

The Supreme Court held that in the murder trial the evidence on behalf of the prosecution of the son or daughter of the victim cannot be discarded on the mere ground of their close interest in the deceased.

State of Rajasthan v. Kalki, AIR 1981 SC

The Supreme Court held that an interested witness is not like approver, only more precaution is necessary.

State of U.P. v. Ballabh Das, AIR 1985 SC

The Supreme Court held that the son of the deceased cannot be disbelieved.

158. Impeaching credit of witness.-The credit of a witness may be impeached in the following ways by the adverse party, or, with the consent of the Court, by the party who calls him—

(a) by the evidence of persons who testify that they, from their knowledge of the witness, believe him to be unworthy of credit;

(b) by proof that the witness has been bribed, or has accepted the offer of a bribe, or has received any other corrupt inducement to give his evidence;

(c) by proof of former statements inconsistent with any part of his evidence which is liable to be contradicted.

Explanation.— A witness declaring another witness to be unworthy of credit may not, upon his examination-in-chief, give reasons for his belief, but he may be asked his reasons in cross-examination, and the answers which he gives cannot be contradicted, though, if they are false, he may afterwards be charged with giving false evidence.

Illustrations

(a) A sues B for the price of goods sold and delivered to B. C says that he delivered the goods to B. Evidence is offered to show that, on a previous occasion, he said that he had not delivered goods to B. The evidence is admissible.

(b) A is accused of the murder of B. C says that B, when dying, declared that A had given B the wound of which he died. Evidence is offered to show that, on a previous occasion, C said that B, when dying, did not declare that A had given B the wound of which he died. The evidence is admissible.

Bhogilal vs Royal Insurance co. ltd (1927) Bom .L.R.

It was held by the privy council that this section should be strictly constructed and narrowly interpreted , otherwise court would have to investigate , on most imperfect materials , questions which have no bearing upon the matter really in contest.

159. Questions tending to corroborate evidence of relevant fact, admissible.-When a witness whom it is intended to corroborate gives evidence of any relevant fact, he may be questioned as to any other circumstances which he observed at or near to the time or place at which such relevant fact occurred, if the Court is of opinion that such circumstances, if proved, would corroborate the testimony of the witness as to the relevant fact which he testifies.

Illustration

A, an accomplice, gives an account of a robbery in which he took part. He describes various incidents unconnected with the robbery which occurred on his way to and from the place where it was committed. Independent evidence of these facts may be given in order to corroborate his evidence as to the robbery itself.

160. Former statements of witness may be proved to corroborate later testimony as to same fact.-In order to corroborate the testimony of a witness, any former statement made by such witness relating to the same fact, at or about the time when the fact took place, or before any authority legally competent to investigate the fact, may be proved.

Ramratan vs State of Rajasthan, AIR 1962 SC

In order to make the former statement admissible it is not necessary that the witness to be corroborated must also say in the court in his testimony that he had made the former statement .

Generally the statements made immediately on the occurrence of an event contain truth , for no time has elapsed for concoctions to creep it..

161. What matters may be proved in connection with proved statement relevant under section 26 or 27.-Whenever any statement, relevant under section 26 or 27, is proved, all matters may be proved either in order to contradict or to corroborate it, or in order to impeach or confirm the credit of the person by whom it was made, which might have been proved if that person had been called as a witness and had denied upon cross-examination the truth of the matter suggested.

COMMENT

The comment mentioned under Section 161 of the Bharatiya Sakshya Adhiniyam, 2023 are based upon Section 158 of the Indian Evidence Act, 1872 (1 of 1872)

In the case of Chandrakala v. Ram Chandra is an incident of alleged rape on a girl by the accused, the girl told her parent that the accuse did a "bad act" with her. By the woras

"bad act" it cannot be said that the accused raped her.

Therefore the court did not believe that the accused raped her and acquired him.

Chandrakala v. Ram Chandra, AIR 1985 SC 1268.

162. Refreshing memory.—(1) A witness may, while under examination, refresh his memory by referring to any writing made by himself at the time of the transaction concerning which he is questioned, or so soon afterwards that the Court considers it likely that the transaction was at that time fresh in his memory:

Provided that the witness may also refer to any such writing made by any other person, and read by the witness within the time aforesaid, if when he read it, he knew it to be correct.

(2) Whenever a witness may refresh his memory by reference to any document, he may, with the permission of the Court, refer to a copy of such document:

Provided that the Court be satisfied that there is sufficient reason for the non-production of the original:

Provided further that an expert may refresh his memory by reference to professional treatises.

Z.B.Bukhari v. B. R. Mehra, AIR 1975 SC

It is immaterial what the document is, whether, it be a book of, account, letter, tradesman's bill, notes made by the witness, or any other document which is likely to assist the memory of the witness. In the above mentioned case the question was whether a candidate appealed to voters on the ground of religion, short and long-notes made by persons who heard the speeches were permitted to be used by them for refreshing memory.

The adverse party has the right of seeing the writing so used and cross-examining the witness thereupon .

163. Testimony to facts stated in document mentioned in section 162.-A witness may also testify to facts mentioned in any such document as is mentioned in section 162, although he has no specific recollection of the facts themselves, if he is sure that the facts were correctly recorded in the document.

Illustration

A book-keeper may testify to facts recorded by him in books regularly kept in the course of business, if he knows that the books were correctly kept, although he has forgotten the particular transactions entered.

State of A.P. Vs Ganeshwara Rao , AIR 1963 SC

A witness testifying to large number of transactions contained in account books or in other documents can be permitted to testify by referring to them.

164. Right of adverse party as to writing used to refresh memory.-Any writing referred to under the provisions of the two last preceding sections shall be produced and shown to the adverse party if he requires it; such party may, if he pleases, cross-examine the witness thereupon.

165. Production of documents.—(1) A witness summoned to produce a document shall, if it is in his possession or power, bring it to Court, notwithstanding any objection which there may be to its production or to its admissibility:

Provided that the validity of any such objection shall be decided on by the Court.

(2) The Court, if it sees fit, may inspect the document, unless it refers to matters of State, or take other evidence to enable it to determine on its admissibility.

(3) If for such a purpose it is necessary to cause any document to be translated, the Court may, if it thinks fit, direct the translator to keep the contents secret, unless the document is to be given in evidence and, if the interpreter disobeys such direction, he shall be held to have committed an offence under section 198 of the Bharatiya Nyaya Sanhita, 2023:

Provided that no Court shall require any communication between the Ministers and the President of India to be produced before it.

State of Bihar V. Kripalu Shanker, AIR 1987 SC

Where the matter in a Government was found to be of privileged character, the matter was held to be not available to support a contempt or defamation case.

> The party claiming privilege may waive it, either absolutely or subject to reservation.

> **In Mantubhai Mehta, (1943) Bom. L. R.,**

The Court for the purpose of deciding whether the claim to privilege is well founded or not is not entitled to look at the document. It must decide the question of the validity of the objection without looking at the document.

Privilege of Newspapers

The privilege of newspaper (known as the news paper rule) protects their sources of information.

X vs. Y, (1988) All. ER

A newspaper reporter collected information from some hospital sources identifying the victims of AIDS admitted there. But the newspaper was permanently restrained from publishing the matter because freedom of the press was comparatively less important than the secrecy of AIDS victims so that they may not be deterred from going to hospitals.

An editor or reporter may be compelled to disclose its source of information, if it is in the interest of public.

166. Giving, as evidence, of document called for and produced on notice.—

When a party calls for a document which he has given the other party notice to produce, and such document is produced and inspected by the party calling for its production, he is bound to give it as evidence if the party producing it requires him to do so.

Liladhar Ratanlal v. Halkarmal (1958) Bom. L. R.

A party is bound to give the opponents documents as evidence in the case if three conditions are fulfilled:

i. the document should be required by that party to be produced in evidence;
ii. it should be inspected by the party calling for its production
iii. the party producing the document should require the party calling for it to put it in evidence.

Emperor v. Makhanlal Datta (1939) Cal.

This section is applicable to criminal as well as to civil actions.

The terms of the Section make it clear that the Section refers to documents asked for by a party during trial. It does not refer to documents produced under O XI, r. 14 of the Civil Procedure Code.

167. Using, as evidence, of document production of which was refused on notice.-When a party refuses to produce a document which he has had notice to produce, he cannot afterwards use the document as evidence without the consent of the other party or the order of the Court.

Illustration

A sues B on an agreement and gives B notice to produce it. At the trial, A calls for the document and B refuses to produce it. A gives secondary evidence of its contents. B seeks to produce the document itself to contradict the secondary evidence given by A, or in order to show that the agreement is not stamped. He cannot do so.

168. Judge's power to put questions or order production.-The Judge may, in order to discover or obtain proof of relevant facts, ask any question he considers necessary, in any form, at any time, of any witness, or of the parties about any fact; and may order the production of any document or thing; and neither the parties nor their representatives shall be entitled to make any objection to any such question or order, nor, without the leave of the Court, to cross-examine any witness upon any answer given in reply to any such question:

Provided that the judgment must be based upon facts declared by this Adhiniyam to be relevant, and duly proved:

Provided further that this section shall not authorise any Judge to compel any witness to answer any question, or to produce any document which such witness would be entitled to refuse to answer or produce under sections 127 to 136, both inclusive, if the question were asked or the document were called for by the adverse party; nor shall the Judge ask any question which it would be improper for any other person to ask under section 151 or 152; nor shall he dispense with primary evidence of any document, except in the cases hereinbefore excepted.

CHAPTER ELEVEN

OF IMPROPER ADMISSION AND REJECTION OF EVIDENCE

169. No new trial for improper admission or rejection of evidence.-The improper admission or rejection of evidence shall not be ground of itself for a new trial or reversal of any decision in any case, if it shall appear to the Court before rejected evidence had been received, it ought not to have varied the decision.

Babulai v. Mohammed Sharif, AIR 1996 MP

A document has been acted upon while pronouncing the judgment and passing the decree in consequence of that, the said document cannot be challenged in appeal in view of this Section.

Talewar Singh v. Bhagwan Das, 1907 CJL

The omission to receive an important document or to examine a material witness justifies a reversal of the decision.

Ramesh Chander Das v. Emperor, 1919 Cal.

When a part of evidence which has been ailowed to go to the jury is found to be irrelevant and inadmissible, it is open to the high Court in appeal either to uphold the verdict upon the remaining evidence on the record under this section or to quash the verdict and order a re-trial.

H. S. Sadashiva v. M. S. Muthappa, 1992 Cr L. J. (Kart.)

When the order according sanction for the prosecution of the accused for non filling of Provident Fund Return was on record but was not marked as exhibit, it was held that order acquitting the accused on that ground was liable to be set aside.

COMMENT

The comment mentioned under Section 169 of the Bharatiya Sakshya Adhiniyam, 2023 are based upon Section 167 of the Indian Evidence Act, 1872 (1 of 1872)

In the case of Narayan . State, it has been held that when the prosecution party is not ready to examine any witness and due to the objection of witness his evidence is not recorded then it cannot be said that a necessary witness was not examined.

Narayan v. State, AIR 1949 SC 484.

CHAPTER TWELVE

REPEAL AND SAVINGS

170. Repeal and savings.—(1) The Indian Evidence Act, 1872 (1 of 1872) is hereby repealed.

(2) Notwithstanding such repeal, if, immediately before the date on which this Adhiniyam comes into force, there is any application, trial, inquiry, investigation, proceeding or appeal pending, then, such application, trial, inquiry, investigation, proceeding or appeal shall be dealt with under the provisions of the Indian Evidence Act, 1872 (1 of 1872), as in force immediately before such commencement, as if this Adhiniyam had not come into force.

Bibliography

THE GAZETTE OF INDIA THE BHARATIYA SAKSHYA ADHINIYAM ,2023 ACT NO 47 OF 2023

www.ingramcontent.com/pod-product-compliance
Lightning Source LLC
LaVergne TN
LVHW070911210926
848482LV00017B/1046
* 9 7 9 8 8 9 5 5 6 2 3 5 2 *